THE **BEAT** GENERATION
IN SAN FRANCISCO

THE **BEAT** GENERATION
IN SAN FRANCISCO

A LITERARY TOUR

"Let's Shout

Our Poems

In San Francisco Streets

–Predict Earthquakes!"

—KEROUAC TO GINSBERG

BILL MORGAN

Introduction by
Lawrence Ferlinghetti

CITY LIGHTS BOOKS SAN FRANCISCO

Cover photograph by Larry Keenan
Book and cover design: Stefan Gutermuth

Library of Congress Cataloging-in-Publication Data

Morgan, Bill, 1949-
  The beat generation in San Francisco : a literary tour / by Bill
Morgan.
     p. cm.
  ISBN 0-87286-417-0
1. Literary landmarks--California--San Francisco--Guidebooks.
2. American literature--California--San Francisco--History and criticism.
3. Authors, American--Homes and haunts--California--San Francisco. 4.
San Francisco (Calif.)--Intellectual life--20th century. 5. Beat
generation--California--San Francisco. 6. San Francisco (Calif.)--In
literature. 7. San Francisco (Calif.)--Guidebooks. I. Title.
  PS144.S4M67 2003
  810.9'979461'09045--dc21

                                        2002041266

CITY LIGHTS BOOKS are edited by Lawrence Ferlinghetti and Nancy J. Peters
and published at the City Lights Bookstore, 261 Columbus Avenue,
San Francisco CA 94133. www.citylights.com

THE BEAT GENERATION IN SAN FRANCISCO

A LITERARY TOUR

"Let's Shout

Our Poems

In San Francisco Streets

–Predict Earthquakes!"

—KEROUAC TO GINSBERG

BILL MORGAN

Introduction by
Lawrence Ferlinghetti

CITY LIGHTS BOOKS SAN FRANCISCO

Cover photograph by Larry Keenan
Book and cover design: Stefan Gutermuth

Library of Congress Cataloging-in-Publication Data

Morgan, Bill, 1949-
   The beat generation in San Francisco : a literary tour / by Bill
Morgan.
      p. cm.
   ISBN 0-87286-417-0
1. Literary landmarks--California--San Francisco--Guidebooks.
2. American literature--California--San Francisco--History and criticism.
3. Authors, American--Homes and haunts--California--San Francisco. 4.
San Francisco (Calif.)--Intellectual life--20th century. 5. Beat
generation--California--San Francisco. 6. San Francisco (Calif.)--In
literature. 7. San Francisco (Calif.)--Guidebooks. I. Title.
   PS144.S4M67 2003
   810.9'979461'09045--dc21

                              2002041266

CITY LIGHTS BOOKS are edited by Lawrence Ferlinghetti and Nancy J. Peters
and published at the City Lights Bookstore, 261 Columbus Avenue,
San Francisco CA 94133. www.citylights.com

For Anne and other travelers

CONTENTS

PREFACE Bill Morgan

I f any city in American deserves the title of home of the Beat Generation, it is San Francisco. Although New York can rightly boast to be the birthplace of the Beats, the literary group came to maturity and national prominence in this most beautiful city by the bay. In the 1950s San Francisco was a magnet attracting inventive writers, artists, and thinkers during the conservative postwar years. Intellectual freedom blossomed with the publication and trial of "Howl" and by the 1960s, San Francisco was the destination of choice for a new generation of radical innovators.

This book grew out of my previous book, *The Beat Generation in New York* published in 1997 by City Lights. Work on that book and other City Lights projects brought me to town so many times that I couldn't resist collecting stories and locations about San Francisco as well. As Allen Ginsberg's photo archivist, I was curious to find the apartment where Ginsberg and Orlovsky took so many photos on Potrero Hill. I wanted to see the house where Jack Kerouac lived with the Cassadys for a season and I wondered what became of the Six Gallery. Unlike many of the "Beat" addresses in New York, most of the buildings in San Francisco remained unchanged by urban renewal. It was a thrill to find Ferlinghetti's apartment where he wrote "Away above a harborful," and searching the backyards of Berkeley for Gary Snyder and Allen Ginsberg's cottages, and walking through the Haight for Michael McClure and Diane di Prima's pads took me to new neighborhoods. Finding the East-West House proved to be a bigger problem than anticipated, but it was solved with the help of former residents like Joanne Kyger, Gary Snyder, and Lenore Kandel. I've become enraptured with the city over the years and through these tours I hope to share my enchantment.

Each of the first nine tours are meant to be possible in an afternoon. Due to the San Francisco terrain, a few of the tours involve significant hills. Wherever possible, I've tried to plot the course that would involve the shortest or easiest climb. But some of the Beat writers would not cooperate and lived on the summits of the San Francisco peaks and there is no way to visit their lairs but to climb, ever upward. Put on your good hiking shoes and let's go!

x

Acknowledgments

This book is truly a collaborative effort. Without the help and advice of a legion of people, it would be hardly more than a pamphlet. First and foremost, I owe thanks to Lawrence Ferlinghetti and Nancy J. Peters. Now in its fiftieth year, City Lights Books owes its longevity to these two editors. They led me through the maze of San Francisco history with a firm and friendly hand, pointing out my wrong turns and setting me on the right path continually. The entire staff at City Lights adopted this project and gave suggestions and advice throughout the course of my research. I owe many thanks to Richard Berman, Elaine Katzenberger, Stacey Lewis, Bob Sharrard and Paul Yamazaki.

Although this is a walking tour to concrete places, the book is really about the flesh-and-blood people who created the Beat movement. To them I owe everlasting gratitude. During my thirty years working with Ferlinghetti and Ginsberg, they opened many doors by introducing me to many of the people who eventually helped me with this book. John Allen Cassady, Neeli Cherkovski, Diane di Prima, and Michael McClure took me around personally, and proudly showed me their town. Ann and Sam Charters, Herbert Gold, Joanne Kyger, Philip Lamantia, Kaye McDonough, David Meltzer, and Philip Whalen generously gave their time to reminisce with me about the past.

Libraries and research institutions also provided a good deal of help with the project. Thanks to Anthony Bliss at the University of California/Bancroft Library, Bolinas Museum, Rita Bottoms at the University of California/Santa Cruz, Dennis Copeland at the Monterey Public Library, Joyce Crews at the Mill Valley Public Library, Gardner Haskell at the San Francisco Public Library/North Beach, Linda Holmes at the Richmond Public Library, the Junior League of San Francisco, Mitzi Kanbara at the San Francisco Public Library/History Center, William McPheron at the Stanford University Library, Mary Ann Miotto at the Palo Alto Public Library, Mary Richardson at the Sausalito Public Library,

Bob Saunderson at the Berkeley Public Library, and Charles B. Teval at the Stanislaus County Library

Photographs and illustrations were generously provided by The Allen Ginsberg Trust, City Lights Books, Philip Adam, Gordon Ball, Carolyn Cassady, Ann Charters, Charles Daly, Christopher Felver, Bennett Hall, Larry Keenan, Chester Kessler, Joanne Kyger, Ed Nyberg, Ira Nowinski, Harry Redl, C.R. Snyder, and Jasmine Stockett, and Beth Sunflower.

Sincere thanks to Terry Adams, Donald Allen, Lisa Brinker, Carolyn Cassady, Gregory Corso, Robert Creeley, Neil Davis, Kate Edgar, Jack Foley, William Gargan, Robin Gaskell, James Grauerholz, Jack W. C. Hagstrom, Peter Hale, Michael Horowitz, Hettie Jones, Kayla Kahn, Lenore Kandel, Eliot Katz, Bill Keogan, Eva Knodt, Shelley Kraut, Robert LaVigne, Amy Evans McClure, Dave Moore, Lorenzo Petroni, Jonah Raskin, Stephen Ronan, Bob Rosenthal, Mary Rudge, Oliver Sacks, John Sampas, Ed Sanders, George Scrivani, Gary Snyder, Robert Sutherland Cohen, the family of Warren Tallman, Anne Waldman, and Ted Wilentz for offering aid whenever needed. In the end, none of this could have been done without the loyal support and love of my wife, Judy.

INTRODUCTION Lawrence Ferlinghetti

A certain young traveler, arriving overland by train and ferry to the San Francisco Embarcadero in the early 1950s, saw a small white city, almost Mediterranean in aspect, a little like Tunis seen from seaward.

He shouldered his sea bag and set foot upon what he saw as truly the last frontier or some temporarily lost Atlantis risen from the sea. He saw the seven hills rising up in early morning light, with small white buildings, sparkling in first light. The hills seemed to sing, and his step was light as he started up Market Street, breathing the bright air, uncertain what direction to take.

On impulse, he stopped the first man he came across and half-seriously asked, "Is this really San Francisco?" The man, swaying a bit, as if he had been lost all night in some waterfront dive, regarded the traveler with jocular eye, tipped his white longshoreman's cap, and let forth a loud guffaw, allowing that this indeed might be the City, but adding "However, young feller, I ain't so sure it ain't necessarily in the U-nited States!"

Thus was he introduced to what he later came to call the original "island mentality" of San Franciscans, including the attitude that the City, surrounded on three sides by water, was indeed an offshore province, not really part of mainland America, rather like natives of Naples who considered themselves Neapolitans first and Italians as an afterthought. It was an illusion that was to be somewhat dissipated in the last half of the century.

The beginning of the 1950s was a germinal moment in the birth of a new America and a new American consciousness. With the end of World War II, hundreds of thousands, uprooted by the war, now returned home briefly, only to leave again, finding themselves adrift in a changed America. Others stayed, married their old sweethearts, and moved to new suburbias. But some—young poets and dreamers, visionaries and vagabonds and wanderers—saw the chance to escape from button-down conformism, consumerism, and boredom. And they began hitchhiking and catching freights, or driving coast to coast, discovering a new America.

San Francisco was the end of the line, and as such it was a natural focal point for the shifting population. It was as if the whole continent had tilted up and poured its contents West. And it took until the early 1950s for any synthesis of a new culture to take form.

In San Francisco, old-style bohemia was still in full flower, its heart being in the Italian quarter of North Beach with its many resident Italian (anti-Mussolini) anarchists.

Renaissance had blossomed in the late 1940s, perhaps centered more in Berkeley than in the City. The literary and political ferment in the City itself was rife with anarchist circles and leftist poetry magazines, much of it gravitating toward the old bohemian district.

Thus it was that North Beach became the place where new literary associations began, and where what became known as the Beat Generation came together: Allen Ginsberg, Jack Kerouac, Gregory Corso, John Wieners, Bob Kaufman, and later Diane di Prima from the East Coast, Robert Creeley from Black Mountain, Michael McClure from Kansas, and Neal Cassady from Denver fell in with West Coast poets Gary Snyder and Joanne Kyger, Philip Lamantia and Philip Whalen, and Robert Duncan and James Broughton. The Beats spiked the Renaissance brew with wild genius, sex, and drugs, and the party was on.

Literature and especially poetry was never the same again, aided and abetted by the local police who busted the City Lights Bookstore on obscenity charges for publishing and selling Ginsberg's epochal "Howl." When the municipal court ruled that the work was not obscene because it had redeeming social significance, the floodgates were down, and New York publishers like the Grove Press rushed into print long-banned works such as Henry Miller's *Tropics* and D. H. Lawrence's *Lady Chatterley's Lover*. It was a legal precedent that has held up to this day, making it ever more difficult for censors to stamp out literature that doesn't meet their prudish standards.

The Beats were like Stone Age hippies, in that they anticipated and articulated many of the themes that became the main tenets of the 1960s counterculture: pacifism and Buddhism, the first voicings of an ecological consciousness, the expansion of consciousness by psychedelics, hedonistic sex and homosexuality, all of which in reality comprised a

"youth revolt" against what was seen as a repressive con-
formist culture.

It would seem that today, in the early years of the twenty-
first century, in a time of increasing American materialism,
militarism, and repression of freedom, America has need
more than ever of the Beat message as detailed in this
prescient book.

ALLEN GINSBERG

HOWL and other poems $1.00

KADDISH and other poems
(1958 - 1960) $1.50

REALITY SANDWICHES
(1953 - 1960) $1.50

PLANET NEWS
(1961 - 1967) $2.00

And now
AIRPLANE DREAMS $2.00

CITY LIGHTS BOOKS

261 COLUMBUS AVENUE SAN FRANCISCO 94133

City Lights Booksellers & Publishers
261 Columbus Avenue (at Broadway)

There's no other spot in San Francisco that embodies the beatific fifty-year history of the Beat Generation better than City Lights Books, still at 261 Columbus Avenue, in the heart of "little old wooden North Beach," as Ferlinghetti called it. It was founded in 1953, the first all-paperback bookstore in the United States, stocking classics of modern literature and progressive politics. In 1956, City Lights published Allen Ginsberg's seminal poem "Howl" and became the lightning rod for a new generation of untamed poets. This rare combination of bookstore and publishing house battles on as one of the increasingly rare, un-chained independent book enterprises in America. Expert bookworms stock a comprehensive selection of the best books in every field. To tell the story of the Beat Generation without mentioning City Lights would be impossible and a walking tour of Beat history naturally begins here. City Lights has been the head, heart, and undersoul of literary San Francisco for half a century, and—as the Gotham Book Mart in Manhattan long ago proclaimed about itself—"Wise Men Fish Here."

The Artigues Building 1.

A lot of cultural history happened within these four walls (one should say these three walls, since the building is triangular). The back of the City Lights building faces Chinatown, while the Columbus Avenue side faces east and looks out on the far end of Western civilization—a fitting location for this crossroads of culture.

Take a look around before going inside. Columbus Avenue was originally called Montgomery Avenue in the nineteenth century, when it was first cut diagonally through the city's rectangular grid system of streets, and has always been the main street of North Beach. In 1906, most everything in this part of the city was destroyed by the great San Francisco earthquake and the fire that followed. This building was no exception. After the firestorm passed and the smoke cleared, the owners rebuilt using the original brick basement arches. In 1907 Oliver Everett designed the new building in Classical Revival style for the French owners, the brothers Emile and Jean Artigues. An Italian bookstore, A. Cavalli & Co. (still in business today at 1437 Stockton), moved into one of the four storefronts a year after the quake. City Lights occupied the same small storefront (at the corner of Kerouac Alley) and then moved into other rooms as space became available in the building. After renting for half a century, City Lights seized the opportunity to buy the building in 2000, retrofitted it to comply with earthquake safety standards, and restored its original appearance. Note the unique clerestory windows along the facade.

As you enter the store, you'll spy a narrow stairway on your right leading to a small mezzanine, used as an office and not open to the public. When you see how precipitous the stairs are, you won't want to climb them anyway. (A sign once affixed to the top said "Watch your step. Many are the fallen women.")

The Mezzanine 2.

It was on the mezzanine that City Lights was born. Peter D. Martin, a native New Yorker, came to San Francisco in the 1940s to teach sociology at San Francisco State College. Martin's father was Carlo Tresca, an Italian anarchist and editor, assassinated in New York City in 1943, maybe by the Mafia. Martin created perhaps the very first pop culture magazine in July 1952. He called it *City Lights* after the great Chaplin film, and published Robert Duncan, Jack Spicer, Philip Lamantia, Lawrence Ferling (a.k.a. Ferlinghetti), and the first film critiques of Pauline Kael (of later *New Yorker* fame). Martin used the mezzanine as his office, above a flower shop once occupying the small entrance room where the cash register is today.

The Triangular Storefront 3.

When the flower shop folded, Martin decided to open a bookstore in the empty space to support the magazine and pay the rent. Lawrence Ferlinghetti recalls, "It was Peter Martin's brilliant idea to have the first all-paperbound bookstore in the country. There weren't any then; there was no place to get quality pocket books." Until that time paperbacks were sold in drugstores and bus stations on spinning racks and occasionally in newsstands or grocery stores. They weren't considered "real" books by the book

trade and bookstores rarely carried them, except for Penguins. (Those literary birds had to be imported from England, since there wasn't yet an American Penguin branch.) At the time, a few publishers were just beginning to experiment with mass-market paperback books. Companies like Signet, Dell, and Avon had been in business for a while, but you couldn't expect to find much selection in the typical drugstore. As Martin was putting up the Pocket Book Shop sign, Ferlinghetti came up the street on the way home from his painting studio on Mission Street, stopped, and introduced himself to Martin, who exclaimed, "Oh, you're the one who sent me the Jacques Prévert translations!" And thus a momentous literary partnership was formed. Ferlinghetti loved the idea of a bookstore since his good friend George Whitman in Paris had started one called Librairie Mistral (later renamed Shakespeare & Co). The little one-room, pie-shaped bookstore opened in June 1953 and Martin and Ferlinghetti began selling new quality paperbacks and early alternative newspapers and magazines. Out front on the sidewalk there were used books in Parisian-style bookracks with lids that could be closed at night (like quayside kiosks in Paris). They had started the store with $500 each, and never dreamed they would take in as much

3

as $50 a day selling paperbacks. Kenneth Rexroth predicted, "There's no way they could ever make a success of that bookstore. Lawrence could stand at the door and hand out paperbacks as fast as he could and he still wouldn't make it." Luckily, Rexroth's pessimism proved wrong. They found they couldn't keep the racks filled or the doors closed. Ferlinghetti said he wanted to sell used books, so that he could sit in the back room, wear a green eyeshade, and read, but he never got the chance. The new paperback revolution was in full swing, and there was no stopping it.

City Lights magazine published only five issues, and, for a variety of reasons, Martin decided to move back to New York. Ferlinghetti bought him out for a thousand dollars in January 1955 and set about working on ideas of his own. From his graduate-school days at the Sorbonne in Paris, Ferlinghetti was familiar with the tradition of booksellers also being publishers, and he wanted to print small editions of poetry in paperback format. City Lights' first publication was his own collection, *Pictures of the Gone World,* published in 1955 in an edition of 500 copies by the fine letterpress printer David Ruff. This was number one of the Pocket Poets Series, inspired by a French publisher's Poets of Today series. *Pictures of the Gone World* was soon followed by *Thirty Spanish Poems of Love and Exile* translated by Kenneth Rexroth, *Poems of Humor & Protest* by Kenneth Patchen, *Howl and Other Poems* by Allen Ginsberg, *True Minds* by Marie Ponsot, and *Here and Now* by Denise Levertov.

PHOTO, © GORDON BALL

SHIGEYOSHI MURAO AT THE CASH REGISTER

Shigeyoshi Murao, a Japanese American born in Seattle, who had spent two years in an Idaho internment camp during World War II, was central to the bookstore from almost the beginning. His personality set the tone for the store. While Ferlinghetti spent much time managing the publishing side, Murao ran the bookstore. In *The Electric Kool-Aid Acid Test,* Tom Wolfe crudely described Murao: "the Nipponese panjandrum of the place, sat glowering with his beard hanging down like those strands of furze and fern in an architect's drawing, drooping over the volumes by the cash register." Never far from him were the *I Ching* and a bottle of Coca-Cola. He told a friend, Gordon Ball, that he was going to call his autobiography *Confessions of a Cokesucker* because he drank more than a dozen a day. Herb Gold recalled that Murao "made an atmosphere that was hugely welcoming and delightful," even if he never kept the books in order or discouraged theft.

The Basement 4.

At the back of the store one day, Ferlinghetti discovered a loose plywood sheet. When he pounded on it, it fell down and revealed a dark cellar that a Chinese electrician used as storage space. This was also the lair of Chinatown's ceremonial dragon, brought out every year for the Chinese

New Year Parade. Ferlinghetti's poem "The Great Chinese Dragon" tells the tale of the dragon "creeping out of an Adler Alley cellar like a worm out of a hole sometime during the second week in February every year when it sorties out of hibernation in its Chinese storeroom pushed from behind by a band of forty-three Chinese electricians and technicians who stuff its peristaltic accordion-body up thru a sidewalk delivery entrance." Ferlinghetti also discovered signs painted on the walls by a Christian sect that had used the basement for prayer meetings, and on the walls today you can still see fragments of them: "Remember Lot's Wife," "Born in Sin and Shapen in Niquity," "I and My Father Are One," and "I Am the Door." Ferlinghetti made a deal with the landlord, put in a staircase, persuaded the Chinese Dragon to leave, and expanded the store into the basement.

Along the stairway to the basement, City Lights installed a letter rack where itinerants could get their mail, as in some French literary cafés. A large bulletin board served as the literary communications center for all of North Beach, with many offers to share rides, apartments, and romance. The

LAWRENCE FERLINGHETTI IN CITY LIGHTS BASEMENT. PHOTO BY LARRY KEENAN

THE BOOKSTORE BASEMENT, 1958. PHOTO, CITY LIGHTS ARCHIVE

basement of the store is what old-timers remember best. They could sit and read without being hassled to buy anything. Here, Jack Kerouac, Allen Ginsberg, Neal Cassady, and other writers read, rapped, and hung out. Neal was often seen roaring up to the store in his jalopy and rushing down here to pick up the latest Edgar Cayce title. Ferlinghetti's "office" was a small room under the stairway (now a storeroom). It was there that Ferlinghetti told Kerouac that his favorite cat had died back home. Not exactly a historic occasion, but Jack recorded his sadness in his most introspective book, *Big Sur.*

The basement is where City Lights "underground" publishing truly began. Their first big break came in October 1955, when Allen Ginsberg read "Howl" at the Six Gallery. Ginsberg had written the poem for himself, never expecting to read it in public, let alone publish it. Ferlinghetti was at the reading and at once recognized Ginsberg as a great new voice in American poetry. He wrote him a telegram echoing Emerson's letter to the young Whitman upon reading *Leaves of Grass:* "I greet you at the beginning of a great career," to which he added, "when do I get the manuscript?" Ferlinghetti did get the manuscript and published *Howl and Other Poems*—and the rest is history. Upon publication in November 1956, there was little attention given to it. Not surprising for a small edition of poetry from a tiny paperback press, a long way from Ginsberg's home turf in New York. But all that changed on June 1, 1957, when

police officers from the juvenile department arrested the bookstore manager, Shigeyoshi Murao—and later Ferlinghetti—for selling *Howl* and the magazine *Miscellaneous Man.* They charged that the material was obscene and would corrupt America's youth. Legal action against Murao and the magazine was dropped, but Ferlinghetti and City Lights were forced to stand trial in the old Hall of Justice. For once, justice did prevail and *Howl* was freed. Judge Clayton Horn ruled that a work could not be considered obscene if it had "the slightest redeeming social significance." This legal precedent was used in later years to publish classics like *Lady Chatterley's Lover, Tropic of Capricorn, Naked Lunch,* and other works of previously banned articulations of the life force in action. The immediate effect of the trial and the accompanying national publicity made Ginsberg's epic poem an underground bestseller and launched a revolution of new "wide-open" American literature. (Pablo Neruda told Ferlinghetti in Cuba in 1959 that he loved "your wide-open poetry.")

Today, poetry has been elevated from the basement and occupies its own room on the second floor and the basement houses nonfiction, with sections entitled Muckraking, Commodity Aesthetics, Topographies, Evidence, People's History, Class War, Stolen Continents, and other mind-shaking categories.

The Main Room   5.

For decades the central room upstairs was rented by an Italian travel agency, Fratelli Forte, who sold steamship tickets back to the Old Country. In 1978 the brothers retired, and City Lights moved in, making the store twice as large and twice as interesting. At that time Ferlinghetti and Nancy Peters moved the publishing branch back to the bookstore after a ten-year stay on upper Grant Avenue, setting up an editorial office in the basement, where Ferlinghetti had worked in the fifties and sixties. In a few years, the editors moved upstairs to the mezzanine, publishing such luminaries as Charles Bukowski, Georges Bataille, Sam Shepard, Karen Finley, and Andrei Codrescu.

WILLIAM S. BURROUGHS SIGNING BOOKS AT CITY LIGHTS, 1980. WITH V. VALE AND PAMELA MOSHER (SEATED). PHOTO BY IRA NOWINSKI

The main room now has the finest fiction by American, English, and European writers, magazines and journals, art books, and City Lights publications. Here and throughout the store, you can find new-release hardcovers and quality paperbacks from all major publishing houses, along with a wide range of titles from harder-to-find small presses and specialty publishers. Each member of the staff has some individual area of expertise and this makes for the inimitable quality of what's on the shelves. The store has always been open until midnight, when some readers intent on spending the night are induced to leave.

At times the bookstore would lose money and the publishing company would bail it out, and vice versa. Thieves were sometimes a problem, too, from gangs of professionals to business-district shoplifters in three-piece suits. Every once in a while a former hippie who'd gone too far with a philosophy of sharing will send City Lights a note of apology and a check to pay for books stolen thirty years ago. Once, one of City Lights' authors, Gregory Corso, smashed in the glass front door after the store was closed and rifled the cash register. People at Vesuvio, the bar across the alley, who saw it happen came over and boarded up the window and called the manager. Perhaps Corso viewed this as an advance on his royalties, and that's how Ferlinghetti treated it. He didn't bring charges, but suggested that Corso might want to get out of town since there were hostile eyewitnesses. Corso split for Rome, where he hung out often in the Campo di Fiori, becoming notorious for his various escapades, and didn't return to San Francisco for many years. (He is now buried in the Protestant Cemetery in the Testaccio district of Rome, near his beloved Shelley.)

The Barber Shop 6.

The next space to be added, up a stair and through a small doorway to your right, was occupied by a certain Ray the Barber. He seems to have augmented his tonsorial income by dealing dope, and was busted, ending up in Soledad Prison. Years later when Ferlinghetti was giving a reading in the prison, who should he see but Ray the Barber, still doing time.

In this room (and elsewhere in the store) you can see many hand-lettered signs by Ferlinghetti: "Stash Your Sell

Phone and Be Here Now." "A Kind of Library Where Books Are Sold." "Free the Press from Its Corporate Owners." "Printers Ink Is the Greater Explosive." "Have a Seat and Read a Book." You'll also find the City Lights logo here and there around the store; it's a medieval guild mark Ferlinghetti chose from the *Koch Book of Signs*. At the front door, he has improved on Dante with a sign that reads "Abandon All Despair, Ye Who Enter Here."

Now known as the Third-World Fiction room, it has books by writers from Asia, Africa, Latin America, the Middle East, and the Caribbean and Pacific Islands. You'll find short story collections here, too, and a rack of literary periodicals. As a young poet, Diane di Prima often sat at a table and wrote down the addresses of all the poetry magazines to which she might send poems. The small alcove in the back has self-published books, books by very small presses, and cutting-edge 'zines. New technologies have now made it possible for writers to design and print their own books, bypassing big-scale distributors, and you're sure to find some results of this exciting self-publishing revolution.

The Second Floor, Poetry Room   7.

One of the last of the old bohemians, Henri Lenoir, founded Vesuvio (the bar next door) and lived in two small rooms upstairs where the Poetry Room is now. It holds one of the largest collections of poetry in any bookstore anywhere. There are thousands of books by everyone from Auden to Zukofsky and there are separate sections for Beat literature, City Lights poets, poetry criticism, and poetry anthologies. Frequent readings, book parties, and signings are held up here, and the schedule for dates and times is posted around the store. There's even a small selection of used books, a small echo of Ferlinghetti's original used bookstore idea. (In fact, the whole store has somewhat the feel of an old used bookstore, since it never attempted to be a "clean, well-lighted place.")

City Lights editorial offices occupy the rest of the second floor. In the 1960s Ferlinghetti began hiring part-time editorial assistants, among them Joanne Joseph, Stella Levy, Jan Herman, and Gail Chiarrello. In 1971, he persuaded Nancy J. Peters (then at the Library of Congress) to work on a special project. He was so impressed with her intelligence and literary savvy that he talked her into working full-time. Later, as director of the company with Ferlinghetti, she became its heart and guiding spirit. Lawrence considered her one of the very best editors in the country. Bob Sharrard began working as a clerk in the store in the mid-seventies and has since become a senior editor and subsidiary rights manager. Elaine Katzenberger, who also began in the bookstore before joining the editorial staff as a talented generalist and first-rate editor, became director of the company in March 2007.

Today, City Lights publishes not only poetry and fiction —including much work in translation—but also books on social and political issues. There are over 100 books in print, and at least a dozen new titles are published every year. The press, like the store, is known for its deep commitment to radical democracy and progressive politics. As former bookstore manager Richard Berman pointed out, "Without the publishing company the store would have been just another bookstore, but working together we have made an impact on American culture."

In 1984, Ferlinghetti made Peters his partner at a time when the business was in serious financial distress; Paul Yamazaki became chief book buyer and Richard Berman store manager. All three had already had over ten years experience at City Lights and they, with veterans Scott Davis, Gent Sturgeon, Andy Bellows, and an outstanding young staff, have made City Lights a great independent bookstore-publisher combination. In recent years, Andy Bellows has become the bookstore manager, Peter Maravelis, events coordinator, has organized many unforgettable literary happenings, publicist Stacey Lewis keeps City Lights in the news, and there's a Web site created by Eric Zassenhaus, covering all aspects of the store—its history, special book stock, mail order department, events, and current news.

On July 16, 2001, the San Francisco Board of Supervisors unanimously named City Lights Landmark number 228 because of its "seminal role in the literary and cultural development of San Francisco and the nation, for stewarding and restoring City Lights Bookstore, for championing First Amendment protections, and for publishing and giving voice to writers and artists everywhere." Now,

CITY LIGHTS WORKFORCE IN 1975. STANDING LEFT TO RIGHT: PAMELA MOSHER, MINDY BAGDON, SHIG MURAO, LAWRENCE FERLINGHETTI, BOB LEVY, AND RICHARD BERMAN. ON THE CURB: CRAIG BROADLEY, NANCY J. PETERS, PAUL YAMAZAKI, SYLVIA, AND V. VALE PHOTO BY BETH SUNFLOWER

after half a century of supporting the right to read, think, write, debate, and dissent, City Lights has come to symbolize the American spirit of intellectual inquiry. From Des Moines to Delhi, people who have followed the fame of City Lights have come to see it with their own eyes. It is still *the* literary meeting place in town. As Ferlinghetti has said, "In a time when the dominant TV-driven consumer culture would seem to result in the 'dumbing down' of America, City Lights is a finger in the dike holding back the flood of unknowing."

CITY LIGHTS LANDMARK CELEBRATION, "DISSENT IS NOT UN-AMERICAN," OCTOBER 28, 2001. PHOTO BY LARRY KEENAN

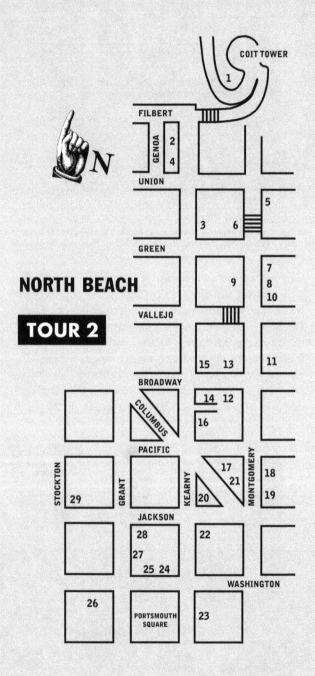

COIT TOWER

1

FILBERT

GENOA

2
4

N

UNION

5

3   6

GREEN

NORTH BEACH

7
8
10

9

TOUR 2

VALLEJO

15   13

11

BROADWAY

14   12

COLUMBUS

16

PACIFIC

STOCKTON

GRANT

KEARNY

17

MONTGOMERY

18

21

19

29

20

JACKSON

28

22

27

25   24

WASHINGTON

26

PORTSMOUTH
SQUARE

23

NORTH BEACH:
Telegraph Hill to Chinatown,
via Montgomery Street

Begin this tour at the base of Coit Tower on top of Telegraph Hill. You can catch the number 39 bus at Washington Square for the ride up to the top, or climb the hill. En route, observe the friendly natives.

Coit Tower 1.

"O anti-verdurous phallic were't not for your pouring height looming in tears like a sick tree or your ever-gaudy-comfort jabbing your city's much wrinkled sky you'd seem an absurd Babel squatting before mortal millions . . ." Thus begins Gregory Corso's "Ode to Coit Tower." The monument shaped like a fire-hose-nozzle erected on Telegraph Hill to honor San Francisco firemen was a gift of nineteenth-century heiress Lilly Hitchcock Coit, who loved the engines (and firemen). The murals inside the lobby of the tower were painted by Work Projects Administration (WPA) artists during the Great Depression. In the fresco entitled "Library" by artist Bernard B. Zakheim at the southwest corner, Kenneth Rexroth climbs a ladder and there's also a book spine with his name on it. Rexroth was the single most important poet and critic of the San

Francisco Renaissance before the Beats arrived in the fifties. During the depression he worked for the WPA and was close to many of the Coit Tower mural artists. Until he moved to Santa Barbara in the 1970s, he continued to exert influence on San Francisco poetics.

Coit Tower was raised in a number of other San Francisco poems. In his 1950s poem "Dog," a mutt's-eye view of the city, Ferlinghetti wrote: "And he goes past the Romeo Ravioli Factory / and past Coit's Tower / and past Congressman Doyle of the Unamerican Committee / He's afraid of Coit's Tower / but he's not afraid of Congressman Doyle / although what he hears is very discouraging / very depressing / very absurd / . . ." Fifty years later, in his 2000 inaugural address as the city's first Poet Laureate, Ferlinghetti recommended that the city tilt Coit Tower. "Think what it did for Pisa!" he exclaimed with tongue firmly in cheek.

As you exit the tower turn to your right and follow the pathway on your right around the back of the tower to the stairs that lead down to Filbert Street on the west side of Telegraph Hill. At the bottom of the stairway, turn left onto Kearny Street and stop at

Richard Brautigan, Nancy J. Peters, and Philip Lamantia's apartments   2.
1427 Kearny / 30 Genoa

In the late 1960s, the young writer Richard Brautigan lived with Valerie Estes in her apartment at 1425 (now 1427) Kearny. Estes was working for Brautigan's publisher, Donald M. Allen, who had moved here from New York after years as an editor at Grove Press. Brautigan's *Trout Fishing in America* had become a national bestseller, and to celebrate, Brautigan painted some very thirsty trout on the toilet seat here.

In 1971 Nancy Peters came to San Francisco on vacation and was so enchanted by the beauty and European flavor of the city, with its multiethnic and sociable neighborhoods, that she decided to move here as soon as she could. When her friend Philip Lamantia told her there was a two-bedroom apartment available in this wooden building for $145 a month, she left her job in Washington, D.C., and moved into 1429 Kearny. Valerie Estes steered her to part-time

NANCY J. PETERS AND PHILIP LAMANTIA. PHOTO BY CHRISTOPHER FELVER

work proofreading Frank O'Hara's *Collected Poems* for Don
Allen. One day on Grant Avenue she ran into Ferlinghetti,
whom she'd met in Paris in 1965, and he asked her if she'd
help edit George Dowden's bibliography of Allen Ginsberg.
Before long she joined Ferlinghetti at City Lights
Publishers. "I hadn't anticipated staying on," she says, "but
manuscripts kept arriving that were irresistible—Kerouac's
Scattered Poems, Neal Cassady's *The First Third,*
Ginsberg's *The Fall of America,* Diane di Prima's
Revolutionary Letters, Julian Beck's *The Life of the
Theater.* I thought I'd landed in some kind of Paradise."

Lamantia was living in the west side of this building at 30
Genoa Place. *[You can see the Genoa side if you turn right
on Union and then right again up Genoa.]* Here he brought
together poems for *The Blood of the Air,* published by Don
Allen at his Four Seasons Foundation Press in 1970. In
1971, Lamantia and Peters joined Allen on a trip to the
Southwest. Making a slight detour, they stopped at Gary
Snyder's place near Nevada City, where they joined the vain
search for the poet Lew Welch, who had strangely disappeared into the Sierras near Snyder's home. No trace of him
was ever found.

Talking with Hopi artists and poets and attending spring
corn ceremonies made a large impression on Lamantia.
Traces of this journey turn up in the poems in *Becoming
Visible* as well as in his manifesto "Poetic Matters," which
urges poets to a "revolt of imaginative power capable of

demolishing any fixed notion of reality." In classes he gave at San Francisco State University and the San Francisco Art Institute during the 1970s and 1980s, Lamantia's subject was "The Poetic Imagination," a dynamic fusion of hermetic arts, radical politics, indigenous worldviews, and pop culture.

Continue walking down Kearny almost to Green. On the left you' ll see

Philip Lamantia and Jack Hirschman's apartments   3.
1314 Kearny

Both Philip Lamantia and Jack Hirschman lived in the same second-floor apartment at different times, Hirschman taking it over in 1978 when Lamantia moved to the old City Lights publisher's apartment. Lamantia was born in San Francisco in 1927, and he lived in North Beach on and off much of his life. In 1942, when he was fifteen years old, a Surrealist exhibition at the San Francisco Museum of Art so turned him on that he began writing poems day and night. At this time, André Breton and other European Surrealists were living in New York as expatriates during the Second World War. When Breton at *VVV* and Charles Henri Ford at *View* magazines accepted Lamantia's poems for publication, he dropped out of Balboa High School and went to New York to join the Surrealists. There he also met Ginsberg, who admired the sensual liberty of his imagination, calling him a "native companion and teacher to myself."

Jack Hirschman, born in 1933, was a native of the Bronx, but has lived in San Francisco since 1973. He lived in this apartment for almost fifteen years, some of them with

PHOTO BY BILL MORGAN

woodcut artist and dancer Kristen Wetterhahn. Hirschman's poems fuse the lyrical and the political. An ardent communist who tries to give voice to the people, he has, as someone said, "taken the free exchange of poetry and politics into the streets." In 1976 he began to write poems in Russian— a Russian poet who was in town read them and remarked, "Jack

KRISTEN WETTERHAHN AND JACK HIRSCHMAN. PHOTO BY ANDRÉ LEWIS

speaks Stalinsky!" Hirschman has made fine, intuitive translations of many great writers, not only from the Russian but from French, Spanish, German, and Italian too. In 2006, he was named San Francisco's poet laureate.

Return the way you came on Kearny and stop at the corner of Union.

Philip Lamantia, Nancy Peters, and James Nolan's apartments 4.
400–408 Union

This is yet another place where Lamantia lived within a stone's throw of the top of Telegraph Hill and it was here that he died in 2005. In 1990, he moved from the City Lights apartment into one in this building, where Nancy Peters had been inhabiting a small top-floor flat since 1974. (Lamantia and Peters were married in Nevada in 1978.) Here, too, lived poet and translator James Nolan, an expansive free spirit and latter-day Beat. He performed with the gender-bending Angels of Light (a group that evolved out of the outrageous Cockettes). On one festive occasion, Allen Ginsberg dressed as a Jewish mamma and sang Blake songs at the Angels of Light Earthquake Cabaret on Gough Street.

Turn right at Union and walk up the hill one block to the next corner. Stop on the southeast corner.

GREGORY CORSO AND SON MAX. PHOTO BY CHRISTOPHER FELVER

Gregory Corso and
Lisa Brinker's apartment   5.
1256 Montgomery

Gregory Corso, considered by many (including Ginsberg) to be the greatest Beat poet of all, was not always the greatest husband and father. Heroin and alcohol habits prevented him from supporting his children or caring for them in any practical way. He was the first to admit that he wasn't cut out for stable, long-term relationships, but most of the various mothers of his children were remarkable women, capable of raising the kids and coping with Gregory. Prospects for his fourth child looked bad at first. However, after the mother took off, leaving the infant boy with Corso, sheer luck brought him an angel, Lisa Brinker, who became Max's adoptive mother. Under her care, Max grew up in a warm, loving environment.

On the southeast corner of Montgomery and Union is a large, pink wooden apartment building where the three of them lived together in the late seventies. Corso liked the ramshackle wooden deck on the roof, where he hung out for hours on an old chaise longue to watch the fog roll in over the bay. In breezy weather Corso and Max flew a kite from the roof. The present penthouse, which now takes up much of the roof, had not yet been built. Gregory was able to afford this spectacular apartment after Peter Coyote helped him get a grant from the California Arts Council. In "For Lisa 2," he writes, "I saw an angel today / without wings / with human smile / and nothing to say."

Brinker, a lovely, serene spirit, inspired many Corso poems.

Go south on Montgomery over the brink of the hill and down the stairs one block to

Gary Snyder & Philip Whalen's apartment 6.
1201 Montgomery (at Green)

The building on the northwest corner of this intersection is where Gary Snyder and Philip Whalen once shared a flat. Snyder was born in San Francisco in 1930, but his family moved away before he was two years old and he didn't return until the 1950s. Snyder and Whalen both graduated in 1951 from Reed College in Portland, Oregon, where they had been classmates of Lew Welch and the anthropologist Dell Hymes. Snyder had taken a few graduate courses at the University of Indiana before moving here to Montgomery Street with Philip Whalen in the fall of 1952. Whalen, born in 1923, had seen action in the Army Air Corps during World War II and went back to school after the war under the GI Bill. After the two young poets moved in here, they took up Asian studies, and worked at various odd jobs—Snyder installing burglar alarms and Whalen doing part-time at the post office. In the summers they worked as fire spotters on lookouts in national forests. (Read all about it in their poems and journals, and in Kerouac's *The Dharma Bums,* as well as John Suiter's excellent *Poets on the Peaks.*)

This building has been heavily renovated since those days. Snyder remembers that their old-fashioned flat was just to the right of the steps at the Montgomery Street entrance. They didn't have heat or a refrigerator and they had to have block ice delivered to keep their food cold. An early poem of Snyder's evokes the time and place: "San Francisco white stairstep-up rooflines. / stucco and tile

21

houses laid out in rows in the Sunset—/ photos after the quake the weird frames of half-broken / buildings. lunch-pails in unfinished walls—how long / since eyes laid on that rafter . . ."

Continue down Montgomery Street to

Peter D. Martin's apartment   7.
1140 Montgomery

Peter D. Martin, cofounder of City Lights Bookstore, was living here when he started his magazine *City Lights* (see Tour One). A year and a half after the store opened, Martin sold his half interest to Ferlinghetti and moved to New York City, where he established the New Yorker Bookstore.

In the same building is

Gregory Corso & Kaye McDonough's flat   8.
1136A Montgomery

Author Kaye McDonough moved to the Bay Area in 1965, supporting herself in temp jobs while dreaming up poems and plays. By 1981, when Gregory Corso moved in with her at this address, she had become a scintillating presence on the North Beach literary scene, with her play *Zelda: Frontier Life in America,* published by City Lights. McDonough had a small printing press in her apartment, on which she handset type for her Greenlight Press. Jordan Belson, a reclusive avant-garde filmmaker who lived in the same building, sometimes complained about the noise from the press, but that was nothing compared to the disturbances that would come after Gregory moved in. McDonough was attracted to the outrageous and often charming Corso, who always seemed to capture the hearts of exceptional women. Just before McDonough gave birth to Nile, Gregory's fifth and youngest child, he wrote "Love Poem for Three for Kaye & Me—and whomever it may come to be." In this apartment Corso also painted a fine portrait of Shelley and Keats that Allen Ginsberg bought and cherished the rest of his life. Corso and McDonough lived together here until 1985, when McDonough decided they'd all be happier if she and Nile moved to Pittsburgh.

GREGORY CORSO AND KAYE MCDONOUGH.   PHOTO BY CHRISTOPHER FELVER

Directly across the street is

Sam Charters's apartment   9.
1131 Montgomery

Before City Lights opened in 1953, Sam Charters was living here, across the street from Pete Martin. Charters, recently discharged from the army after the Korean War, found a job as a Dun & Bradstreet credit investigator, checking out commercial accounts. Friends from New Orleans rented an apartment in Martin's building and Charters soon met Martin there. They talked about his plans for the bookstore, and about how hard it was to get credit to stock even the small space he had found. Charters thought the idea had potential and to help out, he wrote a glowing three-page assessment of its tremendous financial prospects. To everyone's surprise, the venture garnered a triple-A Dun & Bradstreet credit rating that enabled the store to open, and before long Charters's

BOB KAUFMAN, GREGORY CORSO, HAROLD NORSE, AND NEELI CHERKOVSKI, 1978. PHOTO BY MARK GREEN

hunch panned out. Charters loved the jazz clubs of North Beach and pursued interests in both jazz and literature, ultimately writing significant works in both fields. In *Some Poems Poets,* published by Oyez Press, Berkeley (1971), he surveys the famous Beats and also covers such poets as Larry Eigner and Lew Welch, whose importance is often overlooked. Charters lived at this address for only a year or so, then moved on to New Orleans and New York City before returning to the Bay Area in 1956. It was then that he met his future wife, Ann Charters, later a Kerouac biographer and professor specializing in Beat lit. Together Sam and Ann Charters produced Allen Ginsberg's Folkways recording of *First Blues* in 1981.

Continue south down the hill on Montgomery and stop at

Robert Creeley's apartment   10.
1108 Montgomery

Poet Robert Creeley rented an apartment here for $27.50 a month back in 1956 on a brief two-month stay in San Francisco. Besides writing great poetry and drinking heavily, he tried to make money as a blood donor, but was turned down. In the end he took typing jobs with the help of Kenneth Rexroth's wife Marthe. One of those jobs was typing the mimeo masters for the manuscript of Allen Ginsberg's *Howl.* Ginsberg printed up a few copies of it for his friends after the success of the Six Gallery reading. While living in San Francisco, Creeley spent a good deal of time with Jack Kerouac at Locke McCorkle's house in Mill Valley.

Continue south down the hill on Montgomery and stop at

Allen Ginsberg's apartment 11.
1010 Montgomery

Allen Ginsberg lived here from February 3 to September 6, 1955, and it was in this building (before it was renovated) that he wrote much of "Howl." Following the advice of his shrink, Ginsberg resigned from his job in market research, left his girlfriend, and moved to this apartment with his lover, Peter Orlovsky. He gave up trying to live a conventional life and accepted himself as a poet and a homosexual. Ginsberg wrote, "We found an apartment, and it had a room for him, a room for me, and a hall between us; and a kitchen together. So that gave us both a little privacy, and at the same time we could make it when we wanted." Or more exactly, whenever Ginsberg wanted. Although Orlovsky loved Ginsberg, he wasn't gay and was not always open to Ginsberg's desires. They exchanged vows privately, but Orlovsky had many girlfriends over the years and considered himself heterosexual.

During their first summer together, Orlovsky went back to New York to pick up his mentally handicapped younger brother, Lafcadio, who stayed with them on Montgomery Street while he finished high school. Always chronicling the moment, Ginsberg took several photographs of this apartment, certain that someday it would be considered a historic site, and he was right.

Many visitors came to this apartment. Robert Duncan first met Ginsberg here, and Allen remembered Robert carefully studying Kerouac's "Rules for Spontaneous Prose" tacked to the wall. What Duncan remembered, however, was that Ginsberg had nothing on but his underwear and so he was desperate to find something else in the room to look at. He may have read what was tacked on the wall, but he had no recollection of it.

In September Ginsberg moved to a small cottage in Berkeley closer to his classes at the University of California, and the Orlovsky brothers stayed on at Montgomery Street until February 1956, when they moved to Potrero Hill.

A few years earlier, in 1952, ruth weiss, then twenty-four years old, hitchhiked from Chicago to North Beach and moved in to her first apartment at 1010 Montgomery Street.

GINSBERG'S APARTMENT AT 1010 MONTGOMERY, WHERE "HOWL" WAS WRITTEN, 1955.
PHOTO © ALLEN GINSBERG TRUST

GINSBERG IN ALTA PLAZA, 1954.   PHOTO BY CHESTER KESSLER

Like e.e. cummings she decided to do without upper-case letters and has been ruth weiss ever since. She was one of the first poets to perform poetry with jazz at North Beach's famous jazz club, The Cellar. Jack Hirschman said, "Others read to jazz or write from jazz, ruth weiss writes jazz in words." In 1956 she and musicians Wil Carlson, Jack Minger, and Sonny Nelson teamed up at the club for the first time. She loved to write haiku at the Black Cat Café just down the hill. She recalls that Kerouac told her she wrote better haiku than he did.

Turn right onto Broadway. Stay on the right (north) side of the street in order to get the best view of the various locations along the street. Garibaldi Hall is the auditorium in the middle of the block on the south side of the street.

Garibaldi Hall and Mabuhay Gardens 12. 435–443 Broadway

On the south side of Broadway, at 439, is an ornamented building, originally called Dimas-Alang Hall, and renamed Garibaldi Hall after the liberator of Italy. Many poetry readings were given in the big first-floor hall. Allen Ginsberg read what many believe is his greatest poem, "Kaddish," at a 1959 benefit for John Wieners's magazine *Measure*. Ginsberg was joined on stage by Jack Spicer, Robert Duncan, and James Broughton. Later the same year, on August 29, came the "Mad Monster Mammoth Poets' Reading," a benefit for Auerhahn Press organized by Philip Lamantia. That reading featured twelve poets, including Ray Bremser, Lawrence Ferlinghetti, Bob Kaufman, Michael McClure, David Meltzer, and Philip Whalen. (Much of that reading was issued later on a CD entitled *Howls, Raps and Roars*.) Before the reading, two young San Francisco painters, Bruce Conner and Robert LaVigne, staged a "Way Out Walk of Poets" down Grant Avenue to Broadway. Like Pied Pipers in fantastic costumes, they led an immense crowd into the auditorium. Kenneth Rexroth seemed to be the only person not charmed by the event. It was reported that he was in a curmudgeonly mood and spent the whole night muttering to himself, "Awful, awful." Nonetheless, enough money was raised for Auerhahn Press to publish new books by Whalen and Lamantia.

GARIBALDI HALL.   PHOTO BY BILL MORGAN

In the late 1970s the second floor at 443 became Mabuhay Gardens, the Punk Rock capital of San Francisco. Ginsberg, always on the lookout for hot new trends, wrote "Punk Rock Your My Big Crybaby" here in May 1977: "Spank me! Kiss me in the eye! Suck me all over / from Mabuhay Gardens to CBGB's coast to coast." Not surprisingly, Robin Williams called this place "comedy hell" when he was the opening act for the Ramones in 1978.

On the north side of the street about halfway down the block was the

Beach Hotel and Ann's 440 Club   13.
440 Broadway

When Ginsberg arrived back in San Francisco in 1959 to record "Howl" for Fantasy Records, he stayed at the Beach Hotel. In room 27 above Ann's 440 Club, he wrote countless pleas to judges, lawyers, and friends, trying (unsuccessfully) to spring Neal Cassady from San Quentin, where he was glumly serving five-to-life for possession and sale of two joints.

At 440 Broadway, Ann's 440 was a nightclub catering to a lesbian crowd when Lenny Bruce (born Leonard Schneider) was booked here in January 1958 for his first performances ever. The club was still an out-of-the-way joint, even though Johnny Mathis had been discovered here in 1953. Bruce did a Beat sketch about a black hepcat auditioning for Lawrence Welk and another called "Enchanting Transylvania," which is on his first record album. Hugh Hefner caught the act at Ann's 440 and immediately booked Bruce into several Chicago clubs. From this point on, Bruce began a fast rise to infamy. Hounded by censors and the police, this master of outrageous black humor attempted suicide three years later (just up the street). But he still had a long, rough way to go as a "standup tragedian" before dying in 1966 at the age of forty.

Across the street just to the right of Garibaldi Hall on the south side is

Jazz Workshop / Dilexi Gallery 14.
471–473 Broadway

This is the building that housed the Jazz Workshop and the Dilexi Gallery. The Beats loved jazz and often hung out here to catch a jam session. Poet Lew Welch writes about how he'd sit in the Jazz Workshop listening to cool jazz. Tall, thin, and handsome, with a crooked smile, Welch pictured himself as a hip con man. "Those who can't find anything to live for / always invent something to die for. / Then they want the rest of us to / die for it, too."

In 1959 Cannonball Adderley recorded a live album at the Jazz Workshop called *In San Francisco,* helping make it one of the city's top clubs. When the legendary Blackhawk closed in 1963, many regular customers moved here, as did musicians Art Blakey, Ornette Coleman, John Coltrane, Miles Davis, and Sonny Rollins. Lenny Bruce was first arrested for obscenity in this club on October 4, 1961, because his comic sketch about the patrons of Ann's 440 used tough street language.

The Dilexi Gallery was upstairs, above the Jazz Workshop, from 1958 until 1970. Shown here were artists of the San Francisco avant-garde, including Joan Brown, John Chamberlain, Jay DeFeo, Roy De Forest, Richard Diebenkorn, Sam Francis, Sonia Gechtoff, Robert Morris, and Hassel Smith. The gallery closed, its founders said, in order to close the gap between art and life.

On the northeast corner of Kearny is where once was

El Matador 15.
492 Broadway

On the first floor, below today's Green Tortoise Guesthouse, there once existed one of San Francisco's swankiest nightclubs. For a time in the late 1950s the El Matador hosted the likes of Frank Sinatra, Marlon Brando, and Duke Ellington. It was much too pricey for the average North Beach hipster, but in 1959 a special party was given in honor of Jack Kerouac on the occasion of the San Francisco premiere of Robert Frank's joyous film about Beat life, *Pull My Daisy*. That party brought the mainstream celebrity and Beat worlds together. Kerouac arrived at his own party so disheveled that the doorman didn't recognize him and refused to let him in. The film's producer, painter Al Leslie, managed to get him in, only to find that no one at the party had any interest in talking to the author. One of the guests, David Niven, finally noticed what was happening and raised a toast to the guest of honor: "Strike another blow for freedom, Mr. Kerouac!" With that, the ice was broken.

Writer, diplomat, and ex-bullfighter, Barnaby Conrad presided over the place and brought in jazz greats Cal Tjader, Charlie Byrd, and Art Tatum to play here. Conrad wrote about all this in his own book, *Name Dropping: Tales from My Barbary Coast Saloon*.

Turn left on Kearny and stop halfway down the block just past little Nottingham Alley.

Cho-Cho Restaurant 16.
1020 Kearny

One of Richard Brautigan's favorite hangouts was the Cho-Cho Japanese restaurant, once in business here. It could be said that Brautigan lived his whole life upside-down. When *A Confederate General from Big Sur* sold less than 800 copies Brautigan seemed to be on top of the world. When *Trout Fishing in America* sold 2 million he became more and more miserable and fearful of any change that might jeopardize his fame and fortune. His friend Tony Aste had an open affair with Brautigan's wife Ginny, and

Jack Spicer had a crush on Tony Aste (this triangle became the subtext for Spicer's poem "The Holy Grail"). After Tony and Ginny left town, Brautigan and Spicer made Cho-Cho's their preferred hangout. *Trout Fishing* is dedicated to Spicer and another Bay Area poet, Ron Loewinsohn (who later became a professor of English at UC Berkeley).

The Cho-Cho was owned by Jimmy Sakata, one of Brautigan's best friends, and it was from Sakata that Richard borrowed the Smith & Wesson .44 magnum that he used to commit suicide in 1984, at the age of forty-nine.

Herb Gold tells the story of coming to Cho-Cho with the beautiful actress Katharine Ross, star of *The Graduate* and *Butch Cassidy and the Sundance Kid*. When the check came, Sakata had written on it "On the House." When Herb asked why, Sakata said, "If you come with people that look like her, you never have to pay."

Continue down Kearny and at the next corner turn left onto Pacific. Stop on the right side at

Little Fox Theater   17.
535 Pacific (between Montgomery and Kearny)

The Midway Theater at 535 Pacific Avenue was once a small burlesque house with bump-and-grind dancers. In 1961, with materials salvaged from the old Fox Theater on Market Street, the Kingston Trio converted the three adjoining buildings into the Little Fox Theater. From the other side of the street you can clearly see three different buildings and the "Little Fox Theater Building" sign. Ken Kesey's harrowing novel *One Flew Over the Cuckoo's Nest* opened here as a play that enjoyed a long run.

In 1973 Francis Ford Coppola bought the theater and converted it into space for work on *Apocalypse Now* and *The Black Stallion*. Coppola envisioned a future theatrical and film district along Broadway and encouraged other performance groups to use the building. In April 1976 Lawrence Ferlinghetti, wearing a Chaplin derby, read "Director of Alienation" for the first time here. When Coppola's company almost went broke in 1980, he was forced to sell the Little Fox. He took one of the theater seats for his own office (at Columbus at Kearny), but the

RICHARD BRAUTIGAN. PHOTO BY IRA NOWINSKI

theater itself was gutted and converted into the offices that you see today.

Continue east on Pacific and turn right at the next corner onto Montgomery. On the east side of the street you'll see the site of

The Committee Theater 18.
836 Montgomery

As an offshoot of The Committee on Broadway, which staged impromptu, spontaneous, satirical skits, the Committee Theater on Montgomery staged such 1960s plays as Larry Hankin's *The Fool's Play* and Barbara Garson's biting Vietnam-era satire *Macbird.* In 1966

ANNE WALDMAN. PHOTO BY BENNETT HALL

Michael McClure was about to produce his play *The Beard* in another theater, but police threatened the manager that if the "obscene" play were to open they'd rescind his permit. (The climax of the play had a brief scene of simulated oral sex.) McClure then moved the play here, where no such intimidation was anticipated. However, *The Beard* was shut down after the first night on charges of "suspicion of conspiracy to commit a felony." It's farcical that this censorship took place on a block crowded with topless and bottomless strip joints. *The Beard* played in theaters across the country, with frequent closings and arrests, until in New York City it enjoyed a successful run and won two Obies.

Continue down Montgomery one more block and stop at

Black Cat Café   19.
710 Montgomery

One of the earliest bohemian cafés in North Beach, the Black Cat Café opened in this building in the early 1930s in the heart of the old Barbary Coast. The Black Cat was reborn as a fine French brasserie at the corner of Kearny and Broadway for a short time, but the funky original was located here in the beautiful old Canessa Park Building. Clientele of the original Black Cat were Herb Caen, Truman Capote, Kenneth Rexroth, Janet and Charles Richards, William Saroyan, John Steinbeck, and a host of bohemians in black berets and corduroy pants. As some wag said, the place didn't attract writers with drinking problems, but drinkers with writing problems.

In the 1950s, it became a gay club with drag shows and witty cross-dressing skits by Jose Sarria, whose stage name was "The Empress Norton." Ferlinghetti remembers a piano player wearing an old top hat, and a pug dog sitting on top of the upright piano. Alcoholic Beverage Control agents shut down the Black Cat for good on Halloween night, 1963. It has now been recognized as the true birthplace of Gay Pride, where gays were invited to "come out" and be themselves. This was truly revolutionary in the 1950s.

Cross over Montgomery and begin walking up Columbus Avenue to

Bell Hotel   20.
39 Columbus

The Bell Hotel, now gone, was one of the cheap hotels where Jack Kerouac stayed on his frequent San Francisco visits. Look at the old transient apartment building beside it, at 55 Columbus, to get an idea of what the old Bell was like. In *Desolation Angels,* Kerouac talks about the Bell as "A medley of a hotel of rooms in dark carpeted halls, and old creaky night steps and blinking wallclock and 80-year-old bent sage behind the grille, with open doors, and cats . . ." In bed, he listened to the sounds coming in the window—the clatter of dishes, street traffic, and snatches of Chinese conversations—the same sounds you'd hear today. In 1954, Kerouac wrote to tell Allen Ginsberg where to go and what to see on his first visit to San Francisco and

BLACK CAT CAFÉ (AT LEFT). PHOTO BY BILL MORGAN

he suggested the Bell Hotel as a place to find Al Sublette, "the first hep Negro writer in America maybe." Ginsberg and Sublette did meet and became good friends.

Continue up Columbus on the north side of the street and stop in front of number 140, just past the Macaroni Restaurant. You' ll find an entrance to the old cellar covered with a black awning.

The Purple Onion 21.
140 Columbus (between Kearney and Jackson)

One of the legendary cellar clubs in San Francisco was The Purple Onion, run by Bud Steinhoff from 1952 until his death in 1989. The club had been closed for decades but has recently reopened. Legend has it that Steinhoff's original name for it was "The Song Cellar," but Enrico Banducci thought it was a terrible name and told him, "*Anything* would be better than that, even 'The Purple Onion!'" Many entertainers, from the Kingston Trio to Phyllis Diller to the Smothers Brothers, got started here. Rod McKuen, who became America's most popular poet-aster in the 1960s, performed here regularly, but the most prominent writer to work the room was Maya Angelou. As a young poet on the Beat scene in the 1950s, she sang at The Purple Onion long before her book *I Know Why the Caged Bird Sings* made her nationally famous.

Cross Columbus Avenue at Pacific and walk one short block south on Kearny, past the old Sentinel Building, now Francis Ford Coppola's American Zoetrope and Columbus Towers. (There's a plaque on it telling the history.) Stop on the southeast corner of Jackson Street at

hungry i 22.
599 Jackson

Street lore has it that Eric "Big Daddy" Nord ran out of paint while making the first sign for the "Hungry Intellectual" club and it forever remained the "hungry i." Founder Nord, whom Herb Caen called "The King of North Beach," didn't keep the club long. In 1950 he sold the business to Enrico Banducci, who moved it here a few years later from Coppola's Columbus Tower, the building that you just passed a block down the street.

Although Woody Allen, Barbra Streisand, Bill Cosby, Shelley Berman, Lenny Bruce, Dick Gregory, Tom Lehrer, Bob Newhart, Nichols and May, Richard Pryor, Flip Wilson, Jonathan Winters, and the Kingston Trio played here, the man who really made the hungry i was Mort Sahl. In the 1960s Sahl was a satirical social critic who did a lot more than deliver one-liners, influencing a generation of subversive comedians. Eventually the club failed to keep up with the times and in 1968 Banducci closed the club, sold the name to a topless joint on Broadway, and turned his full attention to Enrico's, his restaurant on Broadway.

Continue south and you can't miss the large concrete hotel in the middle of the next block

Hall of Justice site
(now the Hilton) 23.
750 Kearny

The neoclassic Hall of Justice was razed in the 1960s and replaced by this neo-ugly hotel. At one time the Hall of Justice faced Portsmouth Square, which in the nineteenth century was San Francisco's principal public plaza. But the square has been a victim (like the Hall of Justice) of atrocious development design. The massive pedestrian bridge only serves to isolate the area from the surrounding

LAWRENCE FERLINGHETTI, 1957. PHOTO BY HARRY REDL

neighborhood and Portsmouth Square is now more or less the paved-over roof of an underground parking garage. (There's still a graceful monument to writer Robert Louis Stevenson hidden in the northwest corner of the square.)

But to get to the point, the Hall of Justice courtroom over the jail is where the "Howl" trial took place in the fall of 1957. City Lights, defended by the ACLU, with supporting testimony by prominent professors and literary experts, was vindicated, detonating a revolution in American literature and consciousness. Municipal Judge Clayton Horn was a born-again Christian and a conservative judge, but he was always very conscientious and fair. Four years later he also acquitted Lenny Bruce, who'd been charged with obscenity for his trenchant nightclub act. A good view of the old Hall of Justice and Portsmouth Square can be seen in the movie, *The Lady from Shanghai,* filmed in San Francisco around the same time.

Halfway up the block to the west on Washington Street, across from Portsmouth Square you'll find

LAWRENCE FERLINGHETTI AND SHIGEYOSHI MURAO, DEFENDANTS, AT THE "HOWL" TRIAL, SAN FRANCISCO HALL OF JUSTICE, 1957. PHOTO, CITY LIGHTS ARCHIVE

Nam Yuen 24.
740 Washington

According to Jack Kerouac, Gary Snyder's favorite restaurant in Chinatown was Nam Yuen, where late at night after the Six Gallery reading, Snyder brought the poets to sample ginger beef and bitter melon soup. "One of those free-swinging great Chinese restaurants of San Francisco," according to Kerouac. ". . . and he showed me how to order and how to eat with chopsticks and told anecdotes about the Zen Lunatics of the Orient and had me going so glad . . . " Kerouac felt inspired to ask the cook, "Why did Bodhidharma come from the West?" to which the cook replied, "I don't care." This elegant Zen reply pleased Kerouac and Snyder no end and they raised a toast to the cook as a true sage. This restaurant is no longer open, but the Nam Yuen sign remains.

Next door to the left of Nam Yuen is

Sun Hung Heung   25.
744 Washington

Jack Kerouac often looked forward to having a midnight meal at Sam Hung Heung, a modest family-style Chinese restaurant. In *Desolation Angels* he writes that he wanted to walk around the city for hours with a pint bottle, then sit in a booth in this "marvelous old restaurant." Even with Kerouac's remarkable memory, he gets the name of the place slightly mixed up and calls it the Sam Heung Hung in the novel. He describes how he sat on a dark bench in the park across the street and took in the night air: "Drinking in the sight of the foody delicious neons of my restaurant blinking in the little street." The same place has been remodeled several times and is now open as the "Chinatown Restaurant." An early guidebook described the won ton soup as the best in the city, but Kerouac savored "smoked fish, curried chicken, fabulous duck cakes."

Continue west on Washington and cross Grant Avenue to the first building on the south side of the street

Sam Wo   26.
813 Washington

Sam Wo's (sometimes spelled Sam Woh) was a longtime haunt of Beat writers in San Francisco, and one of the few still in business. This very narrow, three-story restaurant will make a big impression on you just as it did the Beats. It might even remind you of a narrow double-deck London bus. On the ground floor, you enter and walk past the Chinese chefs in the kitchen; upstairs you'll find marble-top tables and small stools set in little alcoves, much as

PHOTO BY BILL MORGAN

SAM WO RESTAURANT

it was in the 1950s when the waiter with the unlikely name Edsel Ford Fong presided. He was notorious for being short tempered and authoritarian, often refusing to serve customers what they ordered and bringing them what he thought appropriate. It was all in good fun, or so people hoped.

Michael McClure learned to eat with chopsticks here and Allen Ginsberg liked to have a meal at the hands of Edsel whenever he was in San Francisco. Everyone talked about Sam Wo's, some with ambivalence. Herb Gold said Edsel frightened some people. A. D. Winans brought Charles Bukowski here, and as they walked past the chefs wielding menacing knives and huge meat cleavers, Bukowski mumbled, "I hope the hell you know what you're doing."

Return to Grant and turn north a few doors and you'll spot 916 Grant Avenue on the right side of the street, easily identified by the round doorway.

Li Po 27.
916 Grant

The Li Po bar is still in operation and pretty much the same now as it was when Kerouac, Snyder, Lamantia, Whalen, and Ginsberg frequented it. Inside, a large Buddha still presides over the joint. Perhaps the poets were drawn by the bar's namesake. Li Po, one of China's greatest poets, lived in the eighth century in Szechwan province and, like the Beats, had a taste for wine, poetry, and adventure.

Continue north on Grant to the next corner and turn right on Jackson, stopping at the first cellar entryway.

Woey Loy Goey   28.
699 Jackson

Since 1934 when Woey Loy Goey was nicknamed "The Hole" by its regulars, it's had this basement location. Kenneth Rexroth claimed that Communist cell meetings were held here in the 1930s. One night Ginsberg came in with his friends Shig Murao and Gordon Ball for a late meal. A large German shepherd followed them in and sat down next to their table. The hostess came over, a little annoyed, and asked, "Is this your dog?" Murao thought a moment and pronounced imperiously: "You may take it to the kitchen."

Turn around and go west on Jackson Street up the hill across Grant and stop just before Stockton Street at

S. K. Wong Company   29.
784 Jackson

Film actor and Beat cohort Victor Wong grew up in Chinatown near City Lights as the eldest son of an eldest son. In the Chinese community his father was much respected for his wisdom. He owned a grocery store here that was more a social gathering place than a business. There was an old sofa where people sat and talked about their problems with the elder Wong. Once in the sixties, when Kerouac sensed that he was in deep trouble with alcohol, he asked Victor Wong to introduce him to his wise old father to get some advice. Ferlinghetti and Wong accompanied a tipsy Kerouac, and as Wong describes it in *Jack's Book,* the elder Wong advised, "You know, you should be like the Japanese monks, the Zen monks. You should go up in the mountains, drink all you want, and write poetry." Welcome advice to Kerouac indeed!

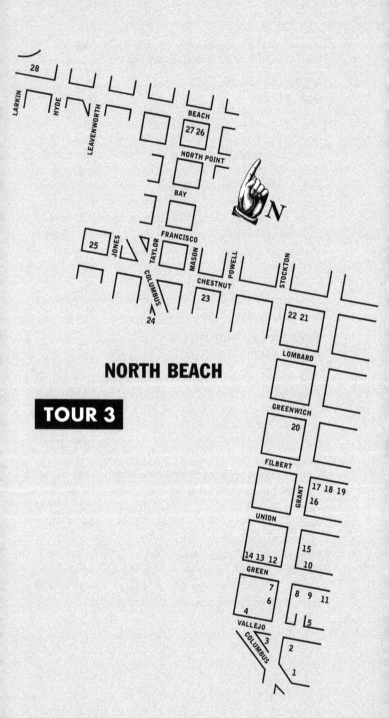

NORTH BEACH

TOUR 3

NORTH BEACH STREET SCENE, CA. 1959. PHOTO BY CHARLES DALY

NORTH BEACH:
Grant Avenue to Fisherman's Wharf

Begin this walk on the wild side in front of the Hotel Europa at 310 Columbus Avenue, which is on the north side of Columbus between Broadway and Grant, very close to the Condor bar.

Hotel Dante (now the Hotel Europa) 1.
310 Columbus

Between 1954, when he arrived in San Francisco, and 1986, the year he died, Bob Kaufman inhabited dozens of dilapidated hotels like this one. In the late nineteenth century these places were built as boardinghouses for working-class Italian immigrants. One dark night in Kaufman's time a fire broke out. Kaufman escaped unharmed but left his manuscripts behind in the burning building. Bob ran into his friend Raymond Foye and told him he'd literally

BOB KAUFMAN ON GRANT AVENUE. PHOTO BY JEFFREY BLANKFORT

survived "Dante's Inferno." Everyone assumed all his manuscripts had gone up in the blaze but that night Foye
slipped under the police barricade and found a scorched
Moroccan leather binder of poems, which he took to the
City Lights office. Ferlinghetti said it felt like they were
entering King Tut's tomb. They laid out the wet pages on
the floor to dry and from those soggy scraps of manuscripts Foye edited Bob's last book, *The Ancient Rain*.

Author Neeli Cherkovski called Kaufman "the ultimate
rebel, the man who lived outside of society. His poems,
however, no matter how keen their social criticism, are
those of a man who yearned to be involved." Kaufman was
the son of a German Jew and an African American Catholic
from Martinique. The prototypical marginal man, he wrote
anarchic manifestos and broadsides and in 1959 helped
found the peripatetic North Beach mimeo magazine
Beatitude. (Someone called it a "floating crap game" since
most any poet who felt the urge could edit it. Issues came
out sporadically, produced in various Beat pads and at the

Bread and Wine Mission at Grant Avenue and Greenwich.)
In 1963, after one of his altercations with the police,
Kaufman took a vow of silence that he kept for fifteen years.
The French called him "the Black American Rimbaud."

*Walk up Columbus to Grant and turn right for one block to the
southeast corner of Vallejo. Stop in front of the former*

New Pisa Restaurant (now Citizen Thai)   2.
1268 Grant

Ferlinghetti wrote, "Not too long / after the beginning of
time / upon a nine o'clock / of a not too hot summer night
/ standing in the door / of the NEW PISA / under the for-
gotten / plaster head of DANTE / waiting for a table / and
watching . . ." The New Pisa is still in existence, but now
a block and a half away at 550 Green.

The old New Pisa was located on this corner and was
famous for its cheap family-style meals. There were a lot of
small tables with checkered tablecloths and one long, shared
table in the center of the room. Gargantuan dishes of minestrone, spaghetti and meatballs, salad, roast chicken, and
jugs of red wine were passed around. Before going to the
Marina for the 1956 Six Gallery reading (which became
famous for Ginsberg's first reading of "Howl"), Kerouac,
Ginsberg, Whalen, Snyder, and Lamantia ate here. When
Herbert Gold first moved to San Francisco in 1960 he ate
often at the New Pisa. One night, he says, a whole group of
Japanese businessmen rose up and sang "Oh Susanna!" to
thank owner Dante Benedetti for his hospitality.

Cross Grant to the southwest corner, where you'll find the

Caffé Trieste   3.
601 Vallejo (corner of Grant)

If you only have time to stop at one café, this is the one.
Since the Giotta family opened the doors in 1956, the
sunny Trieste has changed little. On opening day, a white-
haired coffee maestro from Milan supervised the first few
cups from a shiny new Italian espresso machine. This was
and still is a major writers' hangout in North Beach. Poets
like Gregory Corso, Kaye McDonough, Kirby Doyle, Tisa
Walden, Howard Hart, Allen Ginsberg, Jack Hirschman,
Bob Kaufman, and Jack Kerouac often hung out here,

DICK McBRIDE, SHIGEYOSHI MURAO AND JACK MICHELINE AT THE TRIESTE, 1985.
PHOTO © ALLEN GINSBERG TRUST

yakking late into the evening and sometimes writing. Ferlinghetti wrote a book of one-act plays, *Unfair Arguments with Existence,* at a back table in the 1960s. And Francis Ford Coppola brought a portable tape recorder to work on the script of *The Godfather.*

When a young Neeli Cherkovski arrived in San Francisco in 1975, the poet Harold Norse introduced him to Ferlinghetti here. Cherkovski found an apartment in the alley near the City Lights publishing office on upper Grant and soon became part of the scene. In this café Yippie-turned-businessman Jerry Rubin introduced Cherkovski to his literary agent, who got him a contract with Doubleday for a biography of Ferlinghetti. Cherkovski followed this with *Hank,* a biography of Charles Bukowski. He recalls the day when he and Bukowski were walking past the Trieste and Bukowski paused, looked at the regulars hanging out there, and drawled in a loud voice, "All these guys waiting for something to happen. Only it never will."

Here Harold Norse wrote his poem "At the Trieste" which in part proclaims, " . . .here in San Francisco / as I sit at the Trieste / —recitative of years! / *O Paradiso!* sings the jukebox / as Virgil and Verdi combine / in this life / to produce the only Golden Age / there'll be . . ."

Saturday afternoon the Giotta family and special guests lovingly sing bel canto favorites and belt out arias from Italian opera. The Trieste is still a work in progress, and a chronicle of the place is now being written with the working title of *The Passionate History of the Caffé Trieste.* Its protagonist is Gianni Giotta, "the fisherman's son who came to America."

Across Vallejo, near the corner of Columbus Avenue, you can't miss

St. Francis of Assisi
Roman Catholic Church   4.
610 Vallejo

The French community in the mid-1800s built this lovely Gothic church, named for Italy's patron saint, Francis of Assisi. Perhaps the oldest building in North Beach, it withstood the earthquake and fire of 1906, and the interior has now been restored to its original beauty. A giant beatific statue of St. Francis by Beniamino Bufano once stood at the entrance. Ferlinghetti watched it being installed in 1955 and wrote about it: "They were putting up the statue / of Saint Francis / in front of the church / of Saint Francis / in the city of San Francisco / in a little side street / just off the Avenue / where no birds sang / and the sun was coming up on time / in its usual fashion / and just beginning to shine / on the statue of Saint Francis / where no birds sang / And a lot of old Italians / were standing all around / in the little side street / just off the Avenue / watching the wily workers / who were hoisting up the statue / with a chain and a crane / and other implements . . . ." Before long, however, church officials began to see the larger-than-life statue as a nuisance: it blocked the front steps as people came to masses, weddings, and funerals. And so, in 1961 the statue came down. Poet Bob Kaufman watched from the street that day and wrote a poem called "Afterwards, They Shall Dance": "In the city of St. Francis they have taken down the statue of St. Francis, / And the hummingbirds all fly forward to protest, humming feather poems. . . ." Bufano's St. Francis disappeared altogether for several years, but eventually showed up in a little parking lot at Longshoremen's Hall, near Fisherman's Wharf where you can visit it today. (Gritty pigeons have replaced St. Francis's white doves.)

Jack Kerouac and Philip Lamantia, who both experienced powerful spiritual epiphanies and wrote about them, attended mass here from time to time. In the 1990s Lamantia wrote a moving poem about the charity of St. Francis and the plight of the neighborhood homeless.

When Kerouac's mother came to live briefly in California, he once dropped her off in this church while he went to "score some bread" from Neal Cassady. After Jack and Neal hung out for a while at The Place on Grant Avenue, they finally went back to retrieve Mémêre at her devotions. Nile, the son of Gregory Corso and Kaye McDonough, was baptized in this church. In vagrant moods, Gregory might sit all afternoon on the front steps talking poetry with his coterie and haranguing passersby.

Go back up Vallejo and stop on the other side of Grant at

Stewart Brand's apartment 5.
570 Vallejo

Stewart Brand, the homespun genius and creator of *The Whole Earth Catalog,* lived in number 9 here for several years in the mid-sixties. In 1965, Brand and San Francisco writer Ramon Sender decided to host a weekend festival celebrating the still-legal drug LSD. They called it the Trips Festival, and hired Longshoremen's Hall, asking Bill Graham to organize the event. In January 1966, a few nights before the festival, Ken Kesey and Mountain Girl (one of the Merry Pranksters) were at Brand's apartment. The two spent part of the night on the roof smoking marijuana. Although Kesey noticed several police cars pull up in the street below, he didn't suspect the cops were after them. When the police got to the roof, they struggled with Kesey over a small bag of grass and he was charged with possession and resisting arrest. It was Kesey's second drug bust within a month and carried a five-year sentence, so after the Trips Festival he staged a fake suicide and fled to Mexico. But the ruse didn't rub, and Kesey was put on the

FBI's Most Wanted list. Mountain Girl, who was notice-ably pregnant by the time of her court date, got off with a suspended sentence. Kesey hid out in Mexico for a while before returning to stand trial and served five months before being released on probation. Stewart Brand, one of the most eccentric and original thinkers of his generation, was inspired early on by LSD. One day he came into City Lights Bookstore with a photo of Earth in space and a mad gleam in his eye, asking, "Why haven't we seen a photo of the *whole Earth* yet?" The picture he had in his hand became the famous image for the cover of his *Catalog* and the emblem of Whole Earth enterprises.

Return to Grant and turn right. On the west side of the street in the middle of the block you'll find the

Coffee Gallery   6.
1353 Grant

This spot was always a bohemian hangout, always extremely seedy, and always popular. Originally called Miss Smith's Tea Room, the club then offered Beat enter-tainment, Beat music, Beat art shows, Beat comedy, and Beat poetry. When Leo Riegler owned the Coffee Gallery (before he moved to Vesuvio) he gave young country blues performer Janis Joplin a gig for $10 a night. She was not well received but later, after joining Big Brother and the Holding Company, rocked to immortality. On weekends you'd hear Pony Poindexter or Bev Kelly, and on week-nights poets—among them Bob Kaufman, Lenore Kandel, and Jack Micheline. Even Duke Ellington once blew poetry for a benefit. Both David Meltzer and John Wieners cleaned

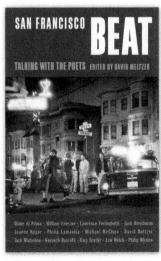

BOOK COVER PHOTO BY JERRY STOLL

up here, but as janitors, not as poets. In its heyday the Coffee Gallery was full of romantic visionaries, spaced-out poets, and boozing locals. *I Am a Lover,* a beautiful book of photos by Jerry Stoll, with commentary by Evan S. Connell, published in 1961 and now long out of print, perfectly captured the character of North Beach and its denizens of that period.

Just next door to this building is a grated doorway,

Shig Murao's apartment   7.
1367 Grant

From 1967 until the mid-1990s, Shigeyoshi Murao lived here. As the manager of City Lights Bookstore at the height of the Beat era, he knew all the poets. Allen Ginsberg, who often stayed with Shig in this small apartment on visits to the city, would sometimes annoy Shig by hanging his socks and underwear out the window to dry. The sound of Shig playing his transverse bamboo flute might be heard at any hour. Ferlinghetti called him an inner-directed and dignified mystic bookman, who often mystified Beat-seeking tourists with enigmatic put-ons they didn't get. He looked like a Japanese sage but had the culture of a hip American. His favorite poet was not Ihara Saikaku but Emily Dickinson. He published irregularly an enigmatic mimeo mag called *Shig's Review.* After suffering a severe stroke, Murao moved to a nursing home near San Jose until his death in 1999.

Directly across Grant is Dupont Thai. Only the old black tiles around the doorway are from the days of the

Co-Existence Bagel Shop   8.
1398 Grant

The Co-Existence Bagel Shop was originally a low-down Jewish deli, but it became the most famous social center for the hobo-boho rebels who swarmed into North Beach in the mid-fifties. Kerouac mentions the Bagel Shop in *Desolation Angels* and it was here that Bob Kaufman waged a small war with the SFPD's "Beatnik Squad," which seemed intent on ridding the city of young "rifraff." His special nemesis was Officer William Bigarani, and at one point in their feud, Kaufman posted a poem by Bill Margolis in a café window, a poem that made clear that Bigarani was Adolf Hitler reincarnated. Kaufman got arrested more often after that and donation cans marked "Bob Kaufman Defense Fund" began to appear around the neighborhood.

Kaufman often improvised poems like "Bagel Shop Jazz," which describes "shadow people, projected on coffee-shop walls . . . mulberry-eyed girls in black stockings, smelling vaguely of mint jelly . . . turtle-neck angel guys . . . coffee-faced Ivy Leaguers . . . whose Harvard was a Fillmore District step."

Kaufman wasn't the only person hassled by the cops at the Bagel Shop; Bigarani arrested Wendy Murphy because she was wearing sandals instead of shoes. A bulletin board served as a news center, with announcements of dances, readings, concerts, and events. But the Bagel Shop never made it economically; the locals nursed their single cup of coffee or beer until the 4 A.M. closing time, and the staff gave away too much potato salad. Owner Jay Hoppe blamed the police: "I am tired of having to deal with a sick city administration and a psychopathic police department," he said as he closed the doors of Beat headquarters on Grant for the last time in 1960.

Turn right up the hill on Green and stop at 481 Green, a building that has been renovated several times.

Gary Snyder's apartment 9.
479 Green (now 481 Green)

Gary Snyder, whom Allen Ginsberg described as "the wildest craziest sharpest cat we've ever met," lived here for less than a year in 1964–65. Just back from eight years in Japan, where he'd studied Buddhism, Snyder began teaching in the English Department at UC Berkeley. To welcome him home, Don Carpenter set up a big poetry reading at Longshoremen's Hall, at which not only Snyder read but also two Reed College friends, Philip Whalen and Lew Welch. It was so successful that Snyder made about a hundred dollars. After stashing some of the money in the oven here, to keep from spending all the loot, the poets blew the rest on a party at Tosca. After Snyder left the apartment in

LEW WELCH AND ALLEN GINSBERG AT CITY LIGHTS, WITH GINSBERG'S POSTER
PROTESTING SOUTH VIETNAM'S MADAME NHU'S VISIT TO THE U.S., 1963.
PHOTO, COURTESY OF THE ALLEN GINSBERG TRUST

1965, Burton Watson, a historian and translator of Asian
literature, used it as a city retreat during the period he
taught at Stanford.

Directly across Green from Snyder's is the

Old Spaghetti Factory (now the Bocce)   10.
478 Green

The old building at this location is one of the few points
on the tour that is actually a designated landmark. The
Bocce Restaurant was originally a pasta factory, long before
Freddy Kuh made it into the "Old Spaghetti Factory" after
the war in the late forties. The entrance then, as now, was
along the narrow pathway at the side of the building leading to a leafy patio, giving the feeling of a secret hideaway.
The exterior is protected from modernization, but peculiar
remodeling has gone on inside.

The Old Spaghetti Factory looked a little like a used furniture store, with an odd collection of junk and painted
chairs of every sort suspended from the ceiling. The enter-
tainment could be anything from flamenco dancing to
chamber music and there was always plenty of beer and jug

wine to drink with the overcooked spaghetti. The management didn't mind if you hung around all evening and drank Anchor Steam; they understood their chef's limitations. (The most loyal diners, and even the cook, admitted the food was terrible.) The Beats hung out here alongside other literati, flamenco dancers, socialites, and tourists. In June 1978, City Lights Books held its twenty-fifth anniversary party here for several hundred guests. Many writers such as Ed Dorn, Robert Duncan, Herbert Gold, Bobbie Louise Hawkins, Bob Kaufman, David Meltzer, and Jack Micheline came to toast and roast Lawrence Ferlinghetti and his staff. At another Spaghetti Factory party, Herbert Gold met Jack Kerouac's daughter, Jan, and they talked about her father. Kerouac had refused to recognize Jan as his daughter, but when she grew up, the resemblance was undeniable. They'd spoken only twice.

Continue up the steep Green Street hill for another block and stop at

Kenneth and Miriam Patchen's apartment 11. 377 Green

Kenneth Patchen was born in Niles, Ohio, on December 13, 1911, but he made his first mark as a poet in Greenwich Village, where he was published by New Directions, the leading avant-garde publisher of poetry after the Second World War. His lyrical-satirical antiwar poetry established him overnight as one of the most important poetic voices of his generation. In 1951 he and his wife Miriam moved to San Francisco. After first staying with friends, fine-press printer David Ruff and Holly Beye, they settled into an apartment here, where he put together the poems published as *Poems of Humor and Protest,* the third book in City Lights' Pocket Poets Series. On publication in 1956, City Lights gave its very first book-signing party, but Patchen (who was living only three blocks away) never showed up. During his San Francisco years Patchen suffered from severe back pain and used a cane to get around town. In search of surgical aid, the couple moved to Palo Alto in late 1956, and after a spinal fusion operation, Kenneth was mostly confined to his bed.

Walk back down Green and cross Grant. Green between Grant and Columbus was (and is) filled with bars, cafés, and restaurants. Most of them from the Beat era no longer exist—The Anxious Asp (528 Green), Mr. Otis (532 Green), Katie's (574 Green), and The Cellar (576 Green). Take a look at the site of one of them.

Anxious Asp   12.
528 Green

This offbeat bar was very Beat. It was run by a New Orleans Creole, Bunny Simon. Kerouac read poetry here, Janis Joplin drank here, and the bathroom walls were covered with pages from the Kinsey Report. Interracial couples felt at home and so did every sort of free spirit. The place resonated with existential anxiety.

A little way down, you'll find a bar that's changed very little.

Gino and Carlo's   13.
548 Green

Poet Jack Spicer came to this bar every day for years. David Meltzer recalled that Spicer would often appear to be passed out at a table, but when the topic of poetry came up he would raise his head and carry on a clear, if rambling, spiel. Young writers like Larry Fagin made the trip to Gino and Carlo's just to sit and listen to Spicer's dissertations. One day Fagin was reading from Chaucer when Spicer came into the bar and began reciting astoundingly long passages from memory. Francis Ford Coppola's "Defense Coordinator" Tony Dingman remembers that one night a young poet approached Spicer at Gino and Carlo's and wanted to know the secret of poetry. Without missing a beat Spicer told the kid to put a quarter in the jukebox and play B25—Johnny Horton's "The Battle of New Orleans." "*That's* the secret of poetry," drawled Spicer. (He didn't miss a beat when he said it, but Ferlinghetti suspected he missed *being* a Beat. He was never one of them and frequently castigated their writing.)

A few doors away is 556 Green. You'll pass the "new" New Pisa restaurant, so you might want to stop in for a look at Peter Le Blanc's woodcut prints of Beat poets. The door right next to the front door of the Caffè Sport was the entrance to

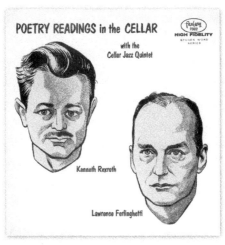

POETRY READINGS in the CELLAR

with the
Cellar Jazz Quintet

Kenneth Rexroth

Lawrence Ferlinghetti

JAZZ AT THE CELLAR.   PHOTO CITY LIGHTS ARCHIVE

The Cellar   14.
576 Green

The Cellar was the underground nightclub in North Beach
that instigated poetry and jazz in the late 1950s. Today the
ghost of The Cellar lies underneath the Caffé Sport. It
opened in 1956 when musicians Wil Carlson, Jack Minger,
and Sonny Nelson converted an old Chinese restaurant
into a nightclub. One night as some jazz musicians were
playing, ruth weiss got up and read poetry. People loved it
and soon the owners publicized Wednesday night as
"Poetry and Jazz Night." On opening night the club, which
held about 100 people, had a line of 500 waiting to get in.
Kenneth Rexroth had been invited to perform with a jazz
backup, so he read his poem, "Thou Shalt Not Kill," with a
free-form jazz accompaniment by saxophonist Bruce
Lippincott. This long tirade (its subtitle was "An Elegy on
the Death of Dylan Thomas") was a precursor of Ginsberg's
"Howl," with its invocation of Moloch and savaging of a
consumer culture that destroyed its poets.

Rexroth picked the little-known poet Ferlinghetti to
share the bill with him, both at the club and on the subse-
quent Fantasy LP "Poetry and Jazz at the Cellar." Rexroth
at the time described the young Ferlinghetti as "a lazy-look-
ing, good-natured man with the canny cocky eye of an old-
time vaudeville tenor." It was Rexroth, a kind of *pater famil-*

ias to the Beat Generation, who set the dissident tone of the jazz-poetry that became emblematic of Beat culture.

Guitarist, folksinger, and poet David Meltzer heard Rexroth and Ferlinghetti and decided to experiment with the form. He arrived with only the outline of a poem and improvised the wording and cadence in sync with the music. Poetry and jazz readings soon spread across the country.

Jack Kerouac said he loved The Cellar. He even dreamed about it high in the mountains during his summer fire watch in the North Cascades: "Because first thing I'm gonna do is hit that otay sweet saxophone Cellar. . . . O they'll all be there, the girls with dark glasses and blonde hair, the brunettes in pretty coats by the side of their little boy (The Man)—raising beers to their lips, sucking in cigarette smoke, beating to the beat of the beat of Bruce Moore

the perfect tenor saxophone. . . ." On May 15, 1956, Kerouac saw Gary Snyder off to Japan and waved good-bye from a dock on the San Francisco waterfront. He and Robert Creeley walked up to The Cellar and celebrated the occasion until they were finally thrown out of the bar by a bouncer who broke Creeley's tooth in the process. Later, Creeley and Kerouac went up to Snyder's old cabin in Mill Valley to stay the night. Creeley brought Marthe Rexroth along (they'd been seeing each other for a while), and Kenneth irrationally took the view that Jack had conspired with Bob to steal his wife. He really never forgave Jack, although he never allowed his antipathy to affect his quite high evaluation of his writing.

LAWRENCE FERLINGHETTI READING AT THE CELLAR. PHOTO BY ED NYBERG

Return up the street to Grant and turn left; in the middle of the block you'll see the

Savoy-Tivoli 15.
1434 Grant

Never a Beat hangout in the early years, there was one memorable reunion reading here in September 1979. At a benefit for *Beatitude* magazine, then-Governor Jerry Brown and hundreds of other poetry addicts turned out to hear Lawrence Ferlinghetti, Allen Ginsberg, Bob Kaufman, Joanne Kyger, Harold Norse, and Peter Orlovsky emote poems. The house was loaded in more ways than one. This was to be Kaufman's comeback after a fifteen-year, self-imposed silence. But Kaufman was nowhere to be found. Just as the show was ending, Kaufman miraculously materialized and vented his "Abomunist Manifesto," with the crowd aiding and abetting. Here's a sample: "Abomunists do not look at pictures painted by presidents and unemployed prime ministers. Abomunists do not write for money; they write the money itself. Abomunists believe only what they dream only after it comes true. Abomunist children must be reared abomunably." Even at a repeat reading later that night, more than a hundred people had to be turned away. Disconsolate souls could be glimpsed at midnight staggering down side streets.

Continue north on Grant for one more block, almost to Filbert Street.

The Place   16.
1546 Grant

In the autumn of 1953, two Black Mountain College alumni, Knute Stiles and Leo Krikorian, opened a friendly bar with funky space to exhibit paintings and give readings, calling it simply The Place. Some of the painters who studied under Clyfford Still and Mark Rothko at the San Francisco Art Institute came here now and then, and they showed work by Wally Hedrick, Robert LaVigne, and Jay DeFeo on the walls. The latter's small paintings were on cardboard, unframed, and priced at a few dollars each. LaVigne's show here was called "The Dangerous Garden of

PHOTO BY BILL MORGAN

Robert LaVigne," where his paintings were interspersed with manuscripts of Allen Ginsberg's poetry. A stuffy art critic at the *San Francisco Chronicle* reported that the black walls of The Place were "covered with modern paintings from the daub-and-swab school," but the locals recognized them as fine far-out visions.

Bartenders John Allen Ryan (director of the Six Gallery) and John Gibbons Langan had picked up the idea of "open readings" from a bar in Chicago. They called theirs "Blabbermouth Night." A yellow soapbox on a balcony at the far end of the narrow room was the lectern for readings, and poets competed for the prize—a bottle of champagne —in something akin to today's poetry slams. Some poets like Joanne Kyger read poems they'd earlier written, while others improvised on the spot. Eccentric and competitive, Jack Spicer was one of the event's biggest enthusiasts, and there was a mailbox into which people could drop submissions to his little magazine, *"J."*

Ginsberg described a typical scene at The Place in his journal on October 15, 1956. "Facing a heavy negro guardian of the gate with his hair bebopped back Chicago Box style poet DuPeru delicate & embarrassed just slipped in at door, black pants & sweater & white shirted over midriff thin skeleton." Other poets who made the scene at The Place included Neal Cassady, Peter and Lafcadio Orlovsky, Gui de Angulo, Hube the Cube, and Bob Donlin.

Jack Kerouac talked about The Place as "his" bar in *Desolation Angels* and *Dharma Bums*. "The Place is a brown lovely bar made of wood, with sawdust, barrel beer in glass mugs, an old piano for anybody to bang on, and an upstairs balcony with little wood tables." When Robert Creeley came to town in 1956, Ginsberg wanted him to meet Kerouac, so he arranged a rendezvous here after he got off work at the Greyhound station. Creeley, who hadn't sorted out Ginsberg's many friends, felt a little nervous because he expected to be meeting the notorious William S. Burroughs, the man who had fatally shot his wife à la William Tell. But on Ginsberg's arrival, the misunderstanding was cleared up, to Bob's relief, and Allen introduced him to Jack. As it happened, the two writers had been watching each other all night but were too shy to say hello. It was a slow way to begin a long friendship.

To the left of The Place at the corner of Filbert was once the headquarters of

City Lights Publishers   17.
1562 Grant

City Lights has always had a shortage of space at 261 Columbus, and in 1967 the publishing operations moved from the bookstore to this building. This storefront served as the distribution center for City Lights publications and (briefly) for other small independent presses. Dick and Bob McBride and Martin Broadley ran this part of the business for several years; in the mid-seventies Craig and Claudia Broadley took it over. In 1978, when the bookstore on Columbus was able to take over an adjoining space being vacated by an Italian travel agency, books replaced Italian steamship brochures in the windows, and the publishing wing moved back to the bookstore permanently. Look for the bronze plaque embedded in the sidewalk on the corner designating this as "Poets' Corner".

Just up the Filbert Street hill around the corner in this same building is the doorway to the

City Lights apartment office   18.
485 Filbert

Before he moved to England to write, Dick McBride secured space for an editorial office here, above the store-

PHOTO BY LAWRENCE FERLINGHETTI

NANCY PETERS AT CITY LIGHTS
EDITORIAL OFFICE, 485 FILBERT, 1974.

front, in a small, three-room second-story apartment. Ferlinghetti was joined here in 1971 by editor Nancy Peters, and together they prepared books for publication and welcomed the many poets and writers and activists who came by. The apartment proved to be a very convenient guest pad for visiting authors, Allen Ginsberg stayed here on some trips to town, arriv-

LAWRENCE FERLINGHETTI AND ANDREI VOZNESENSKY IN THE DOORWAY OF 1562 GRANT AVENUE. PHOTO BY GORDON BALL © GORDON BALL

ing with his harmonium, a small satchel, and a Tibetan bag filled with books. Nancy Peters recalls that after Ginsberg woke up in the morning, he'd always try to meditate for an hour. But each time he sat down, the phone would ring and he'd soon be doing interviews, exchanging poetry gossip, and making plans.

This flat served as Ginsberg's San Francisco center of operations for his investigation proving CIA drug dealing and here he amassed boxes of documentary evidence. Peters says, "Allen believed that ignorance was the root of evil, even the evil of American foreign policy, and so he kept calling the White House and public officials in high places to dispel their ignorance about CIA drug trafficking in Southeast Asia. He'd been calling Richard Helms, then head of the CIA, trying to enlighten him, and Helms actually said he'd look into it and promised Allen that if he found any truth in it he'd meditate every day for the rest of his life. Amazingly, a few days later Helms did call and left a message, 'Please tell Mr. Ginsberg I'm meditating.'"

Michael McClure brought the Doors' lead singer, Jim Morrison, to Filbert Street to meet with Ferlinghetti and the creators of the Living Theater, Julian Beck and Judith Malina, who were stranded close by. After Beck told Morrison about the troupe's difficulties in raising funds to return to Europe, Morrison donated the $2,500 needed for the trip.

CHARLES BUKOWSKI. PHOTO BY SAM CHERRY

Russian poet Andrei Voznesensky visited America in 1972 and during his stay in San Francisco slept on a mattress on the editorial office floor. "The KGB and the CIA kept him under surveillance, they stalked back and forth in front of the building on Grant, just like in the movies," remembered Lawrence Ferlinghetti. Voznesensky looked out the window and saw them and said, "Uh oh, the Control" in his heavy accent. When Peters and Ferlinghetti kidded Andrei about the many female fans trailing up and down the stairs he stated firmly, "Before every reading, I must make love to a woman." He must have had happy experiences, because his readings were always great. Voznesensky told Nancy Peters he intended to write about the tragic 1806 love affair between a Russian explorer, Nicolai Rezanov, and the young daughter of the commandant of the Presidio, Doña Concepción Arguello. Peters had been researching the same story for *Literary San Francisco* and drove him up the coast to visit Fort Ross, the historic Russian fur-trading post.

On a later occasion, Ferlinghetti offered Yevgeny Yevtushenko the use of the apartment, but he required a luxury suite at the St. Francis Hotel. While in the decadent West, he intended to live in appropriate decadence and didn't desire to crash on a mattress in a Beat pad.

One memorable night in the apartment was when Los Angeles writer Charles Bukowski and his girlfriend Linda King stayed here after a reading at the City Lights Poets Theater. When Peters arrived the morning after, she found empty bottles everywhere, a broken window, and a panel kicked out of a door. A contrite Bukowski sat in the wreckage and couldn't remember a thing. Linda King was nowhere to be found. He said she did it. "Women!" he groaned.

Ferlinghetti used the apartment briefly as a temporary home. In 1978 when he and the City Lights office moved out, the Beat Surrealist Philip Lamantia moved in and filled all three rooms, including the kitchen and bathroom, from floor to ceiling with books, continuing the literary lineage at this location well into the 1980s.

Right next to the Filbert Street doorway is

Bob Kaufman Alley (previously Harwood Alley) 19.

Joanna and Michael McClure's first apartment together was a small two-room apartment on the second floor of one of the buildings in this alley. The McClures didn't need much space in the late fifties, because they were usually around the corner hanging out at The Place. One day Michael was stopped on the street by a middle-aged guy in a pirate costume who offered to write a poem for him for a quarter, and that was when he knew it was time to leave North Beach. The guy in the pirate outfit was in fact Paddy O'Sullivan, who dressed as one of the Three Musketeers with sword, cape, and plumed hat. He became a notorious fixture on the North Beach scene, hawking a pamphlet of love poems which he claimed to have written. McClure recalled, "Things looked bad with tourist buses driving through Beatniklandia, and people from the Middle West wearing berets, growing beards, and eating spaghetti while they played bongos in front of bars."

Lawrence Ferlinghetti told the budding poet Neeli Cherkovski that a cheap apartment was vacant at 28

HARWOOD ALLEY LITERARY SALON. KIRBY DOYLE, GEORGE SCRIVANI, NEELI
CHERKOVSKI, RAYMOND FOYE, JACK MUELLER. PHOTOGRAPH BY CHRISTOPHER FELVER

Harwood Alley. In 1976, rentals costing $125 a month
were rare and Cherkovski moved into the three-room
apartment, where he soon presided over a long-running
bohemian literary salon. From time to time, poets Gregory
Corso and Bob Kaufman took advantage of Neeli's generous hospitality and took up residence. Once when Corso
was living there with his infant son Max, Cherkovski's ex-
girlfriend, Lisa Brinker, dropped in to say hello. "Wow!
What a beauty!" cried Gregory. He fell head over heels in
love, and so eventually did she.

The gregarious Cherkovski met often with close friends
Howard Hart, Raymond Foye, George Scrivani, and Kaye
McDonough. He also acquired a reputation for feeding indi-
gent poets when they appeared on his doorstep, so the tiny
apartment grew very crowded at mealtimes. After William.
S. Burroughs's son Billy had a liver transplant, Neeli let him
try to recuperate here. But Billy couldn't stop the heavy
drinking that led to his early death.

Kaufman once told Cherkovski, "When I'm in bed at
night and Billie Holiday is singing the blues outside my

window, and Paul Robeson is singing the Soviet national anthem in my head, and I can't sleep, I go outside and walk the streets of North Beach. And I know I'm home." Kaufman wrote a beautiful poem called "Harwood Alley Song." And Cherkovski wrote an "Elegy for Bob Kaufman"— " 'there is no / third world, / there are / many worlds,' / said Bob / Kaufman on a / political night / around the wobbly / table at / 28 Harwood / Alley. . . ." Ferlinghetti naturally suggested this street for the city to name after Kaufman.

Return to Grant and turn right for one block (up the steep hill) passing Jack Micheline Place on the left, then stop on the south-west corner of Greenwich.

Bread and Wine Mission   20.
501 Greenwich

The Bread and Wine Mission was started by a liberal Congregational minister and writer, Pierre Delattre, who said, "I wanted to have something to write about; so, I decided to spend the first ten to twenty years of my life in social action encouraging what I thought was a very important movement, the counter culture." Encourage it he did! The mission became a focal point for wandering

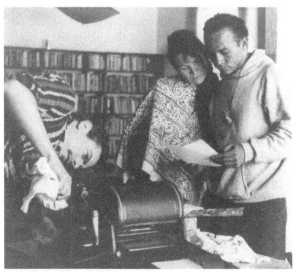

WILLIAM MARGOLIS, EILEEN KAUFMAN, AND BOB KAUFMAN WORKING ON *BEATITUDE* MAGAZINE.

poets and community meals. Joanne Kyger's first poetry reading was here and her friend the poet Philip Whalen came all the way from Oregon to hear it, with a gift of a green pineapple under his arm. Kyger, Whalen, and Robert Duncan formed the Dharma Committee, which met here irregularly. They had crazy rules, like "All members must be depraved once a week." Richard Brautigan, Bob Kaufman, and Gary Snyder read poetry at the mission, to name only a few.

Here Kaufman, John Kelly, and William Margolis found a home in late 1959 for *Beatitude* magazine. Edited and produced at the mission, *Beatitude* was a mimeograph blast begun in May that year with a rotating editorship. It aimed to be "A weekly miscellany of poetry and other jazz designed to extol beauty and promote the beatific or poetic life among the various mendicants, neo-existentialists, christs, poets, painters, musicians and other inhabitants and observers of North Beach, San Francisco, California, United States of North America." All for 25¢. As a weekly, it lasted only five issues, but it continued through the summer of 1960 on a hit-or-miss basis. Since those days it has resurfaced from time to time, whenever some poet felt like editing an issue. Delattre himself wrote poetry for the magazine, but he mostly ministered to those in trouble. *Time* and *Newsweek* were taken by the idea of a "Beatnik priest" and reported snidely on the Bread and Wine Mission in their pages. By the mid-sixties, Delattre had left the mission, become a part-time Buddhist, and moved to Mexico.

Continue two more blocks north on Grant and turn left onto Chestnut to

Lawrence Ferlinghetti's flat   21.
339 Chestnut

Lawrence Ferlinghetti lived here from 1953 until 1958. Visiting the flat was like entering a box of Crayola crayons. His wife, Kirby, painted the rooms of the top-floor apartment in vivid colors; the kitchen was done green to match the avocado tree in the backyard; the dining room was a bright yellow and the hallway a flaming crimson.

In this house he wrote many poems for *Pictures of the*

Gone World and *A Coney Island of the Mind*. *Coney Island* is one of the very few books of poetry to have sold a million copies worldwide. If his publisher, New Directions, had raised the price, he might have become a rich man just on the proceeds, but the price was kept at a dollar for more than a decade. In his poem, "Away above a harborful" he captures

FERLINGHETTI AT CHESTNUT STREET, 1955. PHOTO, CITY LIGHTS ARCHIVE

the view of San Francisco and the sea from here.

> Away above a harborful
> of caulkless houses
> among the charley noble chimneypots
> of a rooftop rigged with clotheslines
> a woman pastes up sails
> upon the wind
> hanging out her morning sheets
> with wooden pins . . .

"Charley noble chimneypots" refer to the vents on the decks of ships such as those Ferlinghetti served on in the navy during World War II. In 1958 the Ferlinghettis found a run-down Victorian on Potrero Hill and moved there.

Continue down Chestnut and stop at the next corner near

Howard Hart's apartment   22.
391 Chestnut

This is the apartment where poet and musician Howard Hart lived with painter-publisher Tisa Walden until his death in August 2002. Although born and raised in Cincinnati, he spent most of his adult life in New York City and San Francisco. He was friends of many writers such as Jack Kerouac and Philip Lamantia and these three poets, along with musician David Amram, performed one of the most important poetry and jazz series at New York's Circle in the Square Theater in the 1950s. These readings directly influenced a generation of poets whose attempts to fuse poetry and jazz often produced inventive uses of language.

Continue down Chestnut another block and stop at the fenced, barnlike structure on the south side of the street.

Telegraph Hill Neighborhood Center   23.
555 Chestnut

The building that houses the Telegraph Hill Neighborhood Center auditorium is just as it was when the City Lights Poets Theater held readings here. This historic community service center was founded in 1890 by social reformer Alice Griffith. The most memorable literary event to take place here was the rare September 4, 1973, appearance of Charles Bukowski. Bukowski was a shy man who hated to perform in public. That night, he sat alone on stage beside a large refrigerator from which he drank one beer after another to calm his nerves while reading from his City Lights book, *Erections, Ejaculations, Exhibitions, and General Tales of Ordinary Madness.* The more he drank, the more hostile he became to a taunting audience who were expecting outrageous behavior, and he began throwing his empty beer bottles out into the room. The listeners responded in kind, throwing the bottles back at him. This genteel literary exercise ended when Bukowski threw his book at the crowd.

Stagger on down Chestnut one block to Columbus Avenue, and on the left at the intersection with Taylor you'll see La Rocca's bar.

Joanne Kyger's apartment   24.
949 Columbus

When poet Joanne Kyger first came to San Francisco from Santa Barbara, in 1957, she was twenty-three. For the first two years she rented an apartment for $50 a month on the top floor above La Rocca's, which looked much as it does today. This was a conservative Italian neighborhood then and the landlord didn't like the idea of a single woman in his building, but she stayed.

JOANNE KYGER, 1965. COURTESY OF JOANNE KYGER

Kyger found work at Brentano's Bookstore in the elegant City of Paris department store downtown and she remembers "taking a lot of Dexedrine and going to the job in my Capezios and Lanz dresses, sitting at a desk ordering books from New York and typing my poems." At night she hung out in North Beach at spots like the Bread and Wine Mission and The Place. It was in the latter that she met poets John Wieners and Joe Dunn, who introduced her to the rest of the North Beach literary gang. Wieners called her "Miss Kids" because she often greeted people with a "Hi, kid"; Spicer wrote a poem called "For Kids" late one night in this apartment. Kyger herself wrote many poems here, including "The Maze," with which she enchanted a group at Wieners's pad one Sunday afternoon. Kyger moved from here to the East-West House in 1959, and then took off for Japan to visit Gary Snyder, whom she would soon marry.

Cross Taylor and continue westward on Chestnut up the steep hill to the corner of Jones and the

San Francisco Art Institute   25.
800 Chestnut

The Art Institute has played a role in literature as well as in the visual arts. It was established as the California School of Fine Arts in 1871, and in 1893 Edward F. Searles donated the Mark Hopkins House on top of Nob Hill for art classes. When that building was destroyed in the Great San Francisco Fire of 1906, the property was sold, and with the proceeds a new art school was built on Russian Hill by the firm of Bakewell and Brown. This Spanish Colonial Revival style building was where, in 1931, Diego Rivera painted a mural to honor American labor. From its earliest days, the school has attracted important artists as faculty: Ansel Adams, Elmer Bischoff, Richard Diebenkorn, Sonia Gechtoff, Ad Reinhardt, Mark Rothko, Hassel Smith, Clyfford Still, and Jean Varda. The poet Robert Duncan's partner Jess [Collins] studied here. In 1953 Jack Spicer became head of the humanities department on the recommendation of Berkeley literature professor Thomas Parkinson. After a year, however, Spicer was let go.

Appointed director in 1945, Douglas MacAgy shook up the school, replacing the Social Realists on the faculty with the exciting new Abstract Expressionists. But when he tried to hire Marcel Duchamp, it proved too much for the trustees, and MacAgy was replaced. During the 1960s the literary faculty included Kenneth Rexroth, Robert Duncan, and James Broughton. Broughton was an important pioneer in both experimental filmmaking and poetry, and he went on to a long and honored teaching career at the school. His films and his poetry were imbued with a whimsical *joie de vivre* and a kind of joyous pathos unique in the history of both media. These qualities also distinguished the two books he published with City Lights, a poetic meditation on filmmaking, *Seeing the Light,* and an autobiographical memoir, *Coming Unbuttoned.* Philip Lamantia gave classes in creative writing here and Ferlinghetti began going to the open studio in the 1980s, drawing from the model and renewing his interest in art.

Go back down the hill to Columbus Avenue and turn left onto Taylor, heading north for three blocks along the cable car tracks to North Point near Fisherman's Wharf. Turn right at North Point and go one block to Mason. Walk left to the corner of Beach and stop in front of

Longshoremen's Hall 26.
400 North Point

This modern Longshoremen's Hall opened in 1959. Eric Hoffer, a radical longshoreman who became famous for his book, *The True Believer,* worked out of here, as did a few other working writers like Lew Welch, who reported here each day for the early morning "shape up." That was where jobs were handed out, so you had to be there to get work for the day. Who knows how many times Welch actually made it after late nights with the North Beach poets. He did make it to the hall for the biggest poetry reading ever held up to that time in San Francisco, the one that became famous for kick-starting the sixties poetry scene. In 1964 when Gary Snyder returned from eight years in Japan, Don Carpenter organized a reading for Snyder, Whalen, and Welch. Eight hundred people showed up to become the largest audience ever gathered for a poetry reading in the city.

The hall also was host in the sixties to the very first psychedelic light show, leading to impresario Bill Graham's famous productions at the Fillmore Auditorium.

The auditorium could hold upwards of 3,000 people, and the first rock concerts were held here, with San Francisco groups like the Jefferson Airplane, the Charlatans, and the Great Society (with vocalist Grace Slick). At one concert, a "long-haired and shaggy-bearded" Allen Ginsberg led a snake dance lasting several hours, according to Ralph J. Gleason's column in the *Chronicle*. On January 21–23, 1966, the union rented the hall out for the Trips Festival, perhaps believing it was a travel agents' conference. Bill Graham produced it, and the Grateful Dead and Big Brother and the Holding Company headed the bill. The Acid Test featured bands, five movie screens, light shows, Ken Kesey with his Merry Pranksters, and the then-legal drug LSD. Neal Cassady, Kerouac's archetypal hero, now known as "Speedlimit" to the Pranksters, dangled "high" above the crowd from the balcony railing. Over

ALLEN GINSBERG AND PETER ORLOVSKY AT AQUATIC PARK IN FRONT OF THE CANNERY, CA.1956. PHOTO © ALLEN GINSBERG TRUST

20,000 people turned out, and the hippie rock revolution was launched. (Some longshoremen would no doubt not have been amused to hear their headquarters called "Longhairmen's Hall.")

Turn left on Beach and return to Taylor. Stop on the southeast corner and see

Beniamino Bufano's Statue of St. Francis 27.
Taylor and Beach

Born in Italy, sculptor Beniamino Benvenuto Bufano had radical anarchist ideas. (There's an alley named after him, off Columbus and Mason.) His concrete statue of St.

Francis was cast in Paris in 1928, before a long and circuitous trip finally brought it here. It was the prototype for a giant 180-foot version that Bufano wanted to put on top of Twin Peaks, like Rio de Janeiro's famous Christ of the Andes, but financial support for the enormous project couldn't be found. In 1955 Bufano's original model was brought to America and placed on the steps of the Church of St. Francis on Vallejo Street in North Beach. It was the subject of poems by Ferlinghetti and Kaufman. But in 1961 the statue was unceremoniously removed from the church and wound up advertising a shopping center across the bay in Oakland. Finally, the Longshoremen offered it a home in this little parking lot. With gentle but rigid arms outstretched, he seems to bless the city as well as all the tourists along Fisherman's Wharf. (Blessing the cars in the parking lot was not among Bufano's original intentions.)

Continue west on Beach Street for several blocks, passing the cable car turnaround. On your right you will find

Aquatic Park and Maritime Museum 28. Foot of Van Ness

The peaceful park and beach below the cable car turnaround is a quiet respite from the throngs of tourists at nearby Fisherman's Wharf. The museum building was originally a bathing casino built in the shape of a triple-deck ship. When that venture failed in 1951, the building became a museum for nautical artifacts. The San Francisco Art Festival was held in Aquatic Park, and in 1954 John Allen Ryan had a booth where he raised money to start the Six Gallery. Allen Ginsberg and his companion Peter Orlovsky posed here on the beach for photos, holding up their favorite cheap wine.

When Bob Kaufman passed on to Beat Nirvana, there was a New Orleans–style funeral parade with jazz band and mourners slowly treading the road between the various Kaufman hangouts and stopping to serenade the present occupants and drinkers with the whole parade ending up at Aquatic Park where two fishing boats took North Beach poets out into the bay to scatter Kaufman's ashes. Just when the boats returned to the dock, a great symbolic rainbow appeared miraculously overarching the rainy skies.

NORTH BEACH

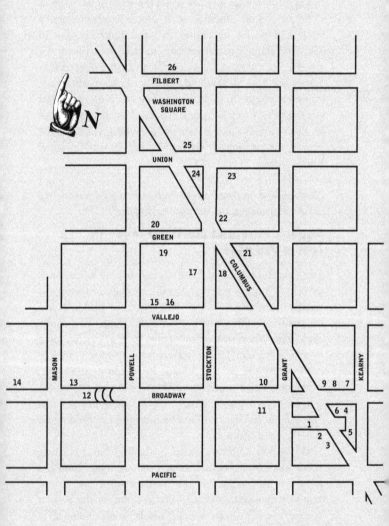

NORTH BEACH:
City Lights to Washington Square

*Begin outside City Lights Bookstore at 261 Columbus, in the alley
called Jack Kerouac Street.*

Jack Kerouac Street and Other Literary
Street Names   1.

On January 25, 1988, San Francisco's Board of Supervisors
approved a proposal by Lawrence Ferlinghetti and City
Lights to rename a dozen streets in honor of the city's lit-
erary greats. At that time, only one half-block alley, Bret
Harte Street, had been named after a San Francisco writer.
Once there had been a Mark Twain Street near Market
Street, but it lasted only a few years before being changed
back to its original name, Annie Street. On October 2,
1988, City Lights staged a celebration of the streets
renamed for Ambrose Bierce, Beniamino Bufano, Richard
Henry Dana, Isadora Duncan, Dashiell Hammett, Bob
Kaufman, Jack Kerouac, Jack London, Frank Norris,
Kenneth Rexroth, William Saroyan, and Mark Twain, all of

MICHAEL MCCLURE, BOB DYLAN, AND ALLEN GINSBERG IN THE ALLEY, 1965.
PHOTO BY LARRY KEENAN

whom had spent much time in San Francisco. This alley between City Lights Bookstore and Vesuvio Cafe is, of course, named for Jack Kerouac. You can pick up a guide to all of the literary streets in the bookstore. We'll also pass Via Ferlinghetti (added—not by City Lights—after the original twelve were designated).

Vesuvio Cafe   2.
255 Columbus

"Don't Envy Beatniks . . . Be One!" said a sign that once hung over the bar here. Vesuvio cashed in on the curiosity seekers who drew up in tour buses hoping to see a Beatnik by selling do-it-yourself Beatnik Kits—sunglass-

es, sandals, beret, false mustache, and a copy of a poem by Paddy O'Sullivan, entitled "How You Gonna Keep 'Em Down on the Peninsula after They've Seen North Beach." Another sign announced: "This is the only genuine Bohemian atmosphere this side of Daly City."

In 1948, Henri Lenoir

opened Vesuvio, his third bar in North Beach. He had owned 12 Adler Alley (now Specs) and was major–domo at the Iron Pot at 639 Montgomery, in a building that no longer exists. Lenoir, an old time bohemian whose real name was Silvio Velleman, was born in a polyglot canton in Switzerland. After moving to Paris, he danced in the chorus of *No No Nanette,* then in the early 1930s landed in Southern California. He loved to spin the story that when his visa ran out, an immigration officer suggested that he just change his name and disappear. (In the 1930s, you could still get away with that!) And so he surfaced in San Francisco as Henri Lenoir. He sold silk stockings to the

HENRI LENOIR, RICHARD HARRITY, SARGENT JOHNSON, WILLIAM RYAN, WING, ALLEN GINSBERG, EVAN S. CONNELL, FLORENCE ALLEN, AND JEAN VARDA AT VESUVIO, 1963. PHOTO TAKEN FOR *COSMOPOLITAN*

ladies in burlesque in the old International Settlement around Pacific Street, just a block from here. Allan Temko, architecture critic and columnist, described Lenoir as kind, witty, and humorous with a "roguish sense of the absurd . . . his bars were spontaneous San Francisco poems, richer, far more delightful, than most of the poems that were read there."

The funky Vesuvio, with its Victorian décor, Beat memorabilia, and friendly staff has long been a gathering place for poets and artists. In the 1950s Dylan Thomas drank too much here on one of his American reading tours, and today you might still find beat-up Beats and errant poets, lost

PHOTO BY IRA NOWINSKI

HENRI LENOIR, LAWRENCE FERLINGHETTI, AND NANCY PETERS.

writers, and wandering film stars. As such, it has always served as a café-annex to City Lights.

In 1960 Kerouac returned to San Francisco hoping to avoid the celebrity circus that had plagued him in New York after the publication of *On the Road.* He thought he'd like to spend serious writing time in Ferlinghetti's remote cabin in Big Sur. The plan was for Jack to call Lawrence from the station as soon as he arrived in town and Lawrence was to pick him up and drive directly to Big Sur, completely avoiding the city and its beckoning bars. But after his cross-country ride, Kerouac came directly to Vesuvio instead, ran into old and new buddies, and proceeded to tie one on. Henry Miller had arranged to drive up from his home on Partington Ridge in Big Sur to Ephraim Doner's house in Carmel Highlands and meet Kerouac for dinner. But Kerouac kept partying and calling Miller every half-hour to say he was about to leave. Finally, Ferlinghetti took off without him and Kerouac and Miller never did meet. Sometime in the early hours, Kerouac took a 150-mile taxi ride to Big Sur, where the taxi left him lost in black night at the bottom of Bixby Canyon. He staggered about with his railroad-brakeman's lantern, looking for Ferlinghetti's cabin in the darkness. At sunrise Ferlinghetti found him stretched out in the tall grass, snoring away.

The antics of some literati were just too much even for Vesuvio. Incised in the cement pavement outside the front door was a list of those permanently 86'd from Vesuvio, among them Paddy O'Sullivan, Gregory Corso, Janice Blue, and Bob Kaufman. The slab has been moved inside.

When Allen Ginsberg was living in San Francisco in 1954, a year before he wrote "Howl," he wrote a poem called "In Vesuvio's Waiting for Sheila," for his girlfriend Sheila Williams. Their relationship ended six months later, after he met his life's companion, Peter Orlovsky.

Just down Columbus a few doors was the

Discovery Bookstore 3.
241–245 Columbus

The Discovery Bookstore was located originally at 241 and later expanded to 245 Columbus. The owner, Fred Roscoe, sold secondhand books and also tried his hand at publishing. He created a loyal following by providing poets and writers in North Beach with reasonably priced used books. David Meltzer worked at Discovery through the sixties and published his own first book, *Ragas,* under the Discovery Press imprint. Meltzer bought a huge book collection from Manny Farber's wife and tried to start his own business, but soon found that he was buying more books than he sold. Obviously, his used-book career didn't last long. Jack Spicer kept his books out of Discovery and City Lights because, as he explained, he didn't want his poetry to be treated as a crass commodity. In fact, he carried on a veritable vendetta against City Lights, which always mystified Ferlinghetti, who didn't dig his poetry but still wanted to have it in his store. "He was a hard man to love," recalls Ferlinghetti, "and so was his poetry."

PHOTO BY BILL MORGAN

Directly across Columbus you'll see

Specs (formerly 12 Adler Place) 4.
12 William Saroyan Place

This bar has long been a hip and funky neighborhood hangout run by

LAFCADIO AND PETER ORLOVSKY, ROBBIE ROBERTSON AND BOB DYLAN, 1965.
PHOTO BY LARRY KEENAN

Specs (Richard Simmons), a genial intellectual and bon vivant. Columnist Herb Caen, San Francisco's Walter Winchell, often came here to catch up on the underground news from the bohemians at the bar. Some say he over-heard Bob Kaufman playing with the words "Beat" and "Sputnik," the Russian satellite—but whoever first coined the word "Beatnik," Herb Caen was the first to use it in print, and it caught on nationwide as an insulting term for the rebellious youth fleeing middle-class conformity. "Beatnik" became a half-humorous, half-contemptuous label that never really fit the Beat writers who were nearly a generation older. But it was a handy way for the straight world to put down the very first dissidents of an evolving revolutionary counterculture that flowered in the sixties and seventies.

According to a recent issue of *North Beach Now*, Specs is still the "Best place to write poetry and the great American novel." If you're looking for subversive inspiration, take a look at the big collection of curiosities—everything from carved scrimshaw and Northwest coast Native American artifacts to a stuffed mongoose fighting a cobra. (Ask the bartender if you can see the stuffed poet in the back room.)

A few steps down Columbus Avenue from Specs is

Tosca 5.
242 Columbus

Tosca, at 242 Columbus, is much more elegant than Specs; it's an old-fashioned after-theater bar with opera on the jukebox (when it's not being blasted by the Hustler Club in the basement). One night Bob Dylan came here with Allen Ginsberg, Lawrence Ferlinghetti, Shig Murao, and Peter and Lafcadio Orlovsky. After a drink, Julius, Peter's mentally handicapped brother, walked into the women's rest room. A small fracas ensued, and the bartender kicked them all out. It wasn't until the next day when he read Herb Caen's gossip column that he learned who he had evicted.

Today, writers, politicians, journalists, and people in film still come here. Sam Shepard, Boz Scaggs, Francis Ford Coppola, and the band U2 like the place as much for the old-time ambience as for the signature drink, cappuccino made with brandy and chocolate. The muckraking journalist Warren Hinckle often inhabited a corner with his patrician beagle in the 1990s and before. The owner, Jeanette Etheridge, has Russian connections, and expatriate Russian artists and literati used to drop in when in town, none of whom looked like they had come from an Evil Empire.

Walk up Columbus past Specs to the corner and make a sharp right onto Broadway, stopping in front of

Mike's Pool Hall 6.
523 Broadway

"I am leading a quiet life in Mike's Place every day watching the champs of the Dante Billiard Parlor and the French pinball addicts." That's the first line of Ferlinghetti's poem "Autobiography." The poem made an impression on a young student in Oregon, Ken Kesey, who fantasized about going to Mike's Place and hanging out in North Beach, just like the Beats. Eventually he made it to Mike's, where he met both Bob Kaufman and a man who became his lifelong friend, Ken Babbs.

Sometimes Ferlinghetti would bring along his dog Homer, who didn't care for pool but enjoyed the minestrone. The prices were right at Mike's. Ferlinghetti remembers the day Kenneth Patchen went in and read the sign over the bar: "Minestrone with meals, 10 cents. Minestrone alone 25 cents." When the barman arrived, Patchen seriously inquired, "How much if you're with someone?"

Go on down Broadway to the next corner, which is Kearny Street. Directly across Broadway you'll see

Enrico's Sidewalk Café 7.
504 Broadway

The owner of the *hungry i* club, Enrico Banducci, moved north to 504 Broadway to create Enrico's, one of the most popular outdoor cafés in San Francisco. It's a wonderful place to sit and watch people promenade along Broadway, despite the traffic. Under new management now, Enrico's was a longtime favorite of Richard Brautigan, who sat at a table on the patio all day long. He said that Enrico's and the Geary Street bus were his two favorite places to think. Frequently he shared a table with his friend Michael McClure, both commenting on the passing scene. Many other colorful characters hung there too, including Barnaby (Bullfight) Conrad, Curt Gentry, and Herb Caen, who put it all in his *Chronicle* columns.

On the back wall of Enrico's the spirit of North Beach bohemia is evoked in Kaffe Fassett's mural, showing patrons and employees of yet another restaurant, the Old Spaghetti Factory, in the 1960s—the poet Thom Gunn is pictured among this merry crew.

Walk back toward Columbus on the same side of the street as Enrico's and stop at

Swiss American Hotel 8.
534 Broadway

The Swiss American Hotel is an old residence hotel that once housed Italian immigrant *paesani*. During the 1980s Bob Kaufman sometimes slept here. One of the hotel's real claims to fame is Lenny Bruce's March 29, 1965, fall from a second-story window. Whether he fell or jumped was never quite known. Bruce was taken to the hospital, where they put his leg in a cast. According to the newspapers, hospital attendants taped his mouth shut to stem the stream of profanity. (He saw it as social commentary.) He

STAMP HELP OUT. IN JANUARY 1963 LENNY BRUCE SENT A TELEGRAM TO CITY LIGHTS, DEMANDING THAT ALL COPIES OF THIS SELF-PUBLISHED BOOK BE IMMEDIATELY DESTROYED BECAUSE HE WAS BEING HASSLED BY CENSORS AND THE POLICE; AND HE FEARED BEING ARRESTED

still had the cast on when Ferlinghetti saw him in the lobby of the old Fillmore Auditorium a few weeks before he passed out from a morphine overdose.

Continue on Broadway past Romolo Alley and stop at the

Marconi Hotel 9.
554 Broadway

When Carolyn Cassady caught Allen Ginsberg in bed with her husband, Neal, she kicked Ginsberg out of their San Jose house as soon as he could put on his pants. That was in August 1954 and Ginsberg took a room at the Marconi Hotel for $60 a month, where he stayed for the next two months. In Ginsberg's *Journals Mid-Fifties* he wrote, "Back alone in a hotel and once again the great battle for survival." With only $14 and no prospects of a job, Ginsberg chose this cheap hotel, which he'd learned about from Al Sublette, who (along with Peter DuPeru) was part of San Francisco's down-and-out scene. Ginsberg liked these street characters as much here as he had in New York, where he'd hung out around seedy Times Square with the likes of Beat hustler Herbert Huncke. Ginsberg described Sublette as an African American seaman, a jazz aficionado, and a friend of Kerouac and Cassady. Ginsberg says he did a lot of reading at the Marconi, everything from William Carlos Williams's *Collected Poems* to Keats's odes. According to Ginsberg's journal, Cassady came by one night and told Ginsberg his Rorschach reading showed that he was "pre-psychotic, sexually sadistic with 'deluded' ideas of reality," whatever that meant.

Continue west on Broadway and cross both Columbus and Grant. Stop in front of

The Committee Revue   10.
622 Broadway

The Committee was an impromptu satirical revue that rivaled Chicago's Second City for cutting-edge humor and absurd wit. In the mid-1960s it satirized middle-class American morality with a vengeance. Committee numbers were partially rehearsed yet seemed entirely improvised. You never knew what to expect, except that they would be irreverent and sometimes hilarious. Herb Gold said that the change from the Beatnik to the hippie era could be marked for him the night The Committee used the word "uptight" three or four times. He had never heard the

PETER DUPERU, NEAL CASSADY, AND NATALIE JACKSON AT BROADWAY TUNNEL (NOTE ALFRED'S SIGN), 1955.   PHOTO © ALLEN GINSBERG TRUST

expression before. "Don't be so uptight!" became a signature phrase of a new "let it all hang out" epoch.

In the mid-seventies, Anne Waldman read her "Fast Speaking Woman" at The Committee. She remembered being nervous and jangled. "The space was large, a daunting crowd, many friends. I had this long litany which required nerve, speed, rhythmic heartbeat, lyrical push." After her dynamic reading, Ferlinghetti asked to publish the poems, which had been inspired by the ritual chants of the Mexican shaman Maria Sabina. It became number thirty-three in the Pocket Poets Series.

Directly across Broadway from The Committee is the

Colombo Hotel (now the Sam Wong Hotel) 11. 615 Broadway

The Sam Wong Hotel is the spruced-up version of the old Colombo Hotel, where early City Lights Bookstore manager Shig Murao lived from 1955 to 1962. This was his home when he was arrested for selling cops a copy of Allen Ginsberg's *Howl and Other Poems*. In later years, looking back on the *Howl* bust, Murao would say to friends, "Just imagine, being arrested for selling poetry!"

Walk west on Broadway for two more blocks and stop on the corner of Powell in front of the

Broadway Tunnel 12. Broadway between Powell and Larkin

Broadway cuts underneath Russian Hill just to the west of Powell. Allen Ginsberg and his friends often walked through the tunnel on their way to and from his apartment in Polk Gulch. Kerouac wrote, "We buy cantaloupes and grapes and split and walk down across the Broadway Tunnel yelling in loud voices to make the echo, munching grapes and slobbering at cantaloupes and throwing them away . . ." It's the same tunnel in which Jack Spicer was seriously injured in a car crash.

Don't go into the tunnel but continue up the hill on the right almost to Mason to the building at 886 Broadway.

Alfred's Restaurant   13.
886 Broadway

In *On the Road* Kerouac describes a lavish dinner he and his prep school classmate Henri Cru had at Alfred's, then a landmark at 886 Broadway. The cost was all of $10 per person, which was a staggering sum in 1947, perhaps equivalent to $150 today. It was Kerouac's first trip to California and he was staying with Cru in Marin County. When Cru's father came to town on a business trip, he took them to a fancy dinner here. Another of Kerouac's friends from his college days at Columbia, Allan Temko, just happened to be at the bar. He was crocked, as Kerouac put it. Temko insulted Cru's father and unable to control himself, Kerouac started drinking too, even though he feared Cru might never speak to him again. Everyone always forgave Kerouac and Cru was no exception. Although the restaurant is gone, the building is still pretty much the same. Allen Ginsberg captured Alfred's large sign in the background of a photograph he took of friends Peter DuPeru, Neal Cassady, and Neal's girlfriend Natalie Jackson on the street in front of the tunnel.

Continue up the steep Broadway hill to

David Ruff and Holly Beye's house   14.
970 Broadway

The printer David Ruff and his wife, poet Holly Beye, lived in the little wooden house at this address, up the hill from Alfred's Restaurant. Beye was a friend of Ferlinghetti's wife, Kirby, who had gone to Swarthmore with her. The two couples got together when the Ferlinghettis first settled in San Francisco in the early fifties. David and Holly shared Lawrence's anarchist political sympathies and it was Ruff who set the type for Ferlinghetti's first book, *Pictures of the Gone World*. The two couples worked together, assembling the books for sale in the bookstore at sixty-five cents a copy.

Go back down the hill to Mason and turn left one block to Vallejo, then right one block, crossing Powell. There, you'll see the

North Beach Police Station   15.
766 Vallejo

The North Beach Police Station played a dim part in the lives of several Beat writers. In 1957, a newspaper headline summed it up: "Cops Don't Allow No Renaissance Here." Police kept tabs on the writers and were quick to arrest them for being "under the influence." The poets regarded the arrests as harassment and were suspicious of all activities in this building.

Once in the late 1970s, Ferlinghetti went to the North Beach station to get a release for an abandoned car that had been towed. He'd given his ancient VW bug to City Lights staffer Paul Yamazaki, who had lost track of it. At the station house the police ran a check and found an old warrant out on Ferlinghetti for "sex crimes" and he was taken to jail. Nancy Peters went down to bail him out. The warrant had been issued ten years earlier for the "crime" of selling *The Love Book,* a volume of erotic poetry by Lenore Kandel. The case had been thrown out of court at the time, but the lawyer had neglected to get the record cleared. Ferlinghetti went to court the next morning and the judge dismissed the case.

A little farther east along Vallejo you'll cross an alley to

Keystone Korner (now the Little Garden restaurant)   16.
750 Vallejo

Keystone Korner was an important venue for some of the biggest names in jazz. In addition to musicians like Zoot Sims, Bill Evans, and the Dexter Gordon Quartet, Keystone also had poetry readings with jazz backup, and Ferlinghetti read there with various musicians, most of whom he thought were too stoned to pay much attention to his poetry.

For decades, William S. Burroughs lived an expatriate life in Mexico, Europe, and Morocco. He didn't make it to San Francisco until March 1981, when he was welcomed with standing-room-only crowds each night of his readings at Keystone Korner. On that visit Burroughs met V. Vale, the editor of the punk tabloid *Search & Destroy,* and "their association led to the mutation of *Re/Search* as both a magazine and a publishing company," according to Burroughs's assistant, James Grauerholz. After a long series of readings organized by Nathan May, Keystone Korner closed in 1983, the victim of changing times and various drug habits. It was the last of the great old live jazz clubs like the Jazz Workshop and The Blue Note.

Continue down Vallejo to Stockton, then turn left for a half block and stop at the

North Beach Museum (on the second floor of the US Bank)   17.
1435 Stockton

The North Beach Museum fits on the mezzanine of the US Bank. It's devoted to North Beach history and there is a lovely manuscript on display of Lawrence Ferlinghetti's handwritten poem, "The Old Italians Dying." That poem records the passing of a generation of North Beach Italian immigrants.

Across Stockton at the corner of Columbus is the triangular building now housing the Panta Rei restaurant

U.S. Restaurant / Fitz Hugh Ludlow Memorial Library   18.
431 Columbus / 451 Columbus

For more than half a century the much beloved neighborhood eatery, the U.S. Restaurant, was located at 431 Columbus, at the corner of Stockton. "U.S." does not stand for United States, as most people assume, but for Unione Sportiva, a nineteenth-century Italian sports club, and inside the old U.S., bocce ball trophies and old photos of local Italian sports teams were proudly displayed.

Twenty years ago Gregory Corso and Neeli Cherkovski were eating here when a couple of cops came in and took seats at their large table. Corso thought it a fine opportunity to let them know how unfair he thought United States drug laws were. As he became more and more belligerent, pounding the table to make a point, a minor earthquake hit the city and plaster began to rain down on everyone. Corso had called down retribution.

ALLEN GINSBERG AND GREGORY CORSO. PHOTO BY CHRISTOPHER FELVER

Ferlinghetti's picture can be seen, along with images of family members, in the mural on the wall of the new U.S. at 515 Columbus, just down the street.

The second floor of this building housed the Fitz Hugh Ludlow Memorial Library during the early seventies, in an office at the prow of the building. The country's largest independent reference collection on psychedelic drugs, the library was begun in 1970 when Michael Horowitz, Robert Barker, and William Dailey combined their personal collections and made them available for study and research. They named it after Fitz Hugh Ludlow, the erudite nineteenth-century American who wrote a book extolling marijuana, *The Hasheesh Eater: Being Passages from the Life of a Pythagorean* (1857). In 1863 Ludlow visited San Francisco, wrote for the local literary journals, and befriended Mark Twain. Known as the American De Quincey, he became a cult figure after his book was published. (His gravestone could have read "Ludlow lauded laudanum.")

Psychedelic guru Timothy Leary's archives were secretly housed in the Ludlow Library while he was in prison and during his later fugitive years. Allen Ginsberg was a frequent visitor to the library, and he spearheaded a battle to free Leary from prison. It was here, on July 4, 1971, that Ginsberg wrote his *Declaration of Independence for Timothy Leary*. The campaign was ultimately successful.

CITY LIGHTS PARTY AT THE OLD SPAGHETTI FACTORY. PHOTO BY IRA NOWINSKI

Turn left on Green Street and walk half a block, where you'll see

Green Street Mortuary 19.
649 Green

If you are lucky enough to see a funeral procession led by an old-fashioned brass marching band on the streets of North Beach, it will have originated here. Ferlinghetti captured its spirit in the poem, "The Green Street Mortuary Marching Band" (published in *A Far Rockaway of the Heart*). Jessica Mitford, famous for her satiric *The American Way of Death*, arranged for an elegant old funeral carriage drawn by a team of black horses to be accompanied by the Green Street Mortuary Marching Band after her memorial service.

On the other side of Green Street you'll see the Italianate

Fugazi Hall 20.
678 Green

When John Fugazi, a founder of the Transamerica Company, donated Casa Coloniale Italiana (now Fugazi Hall) to the community in 1912 he probably would have been astounded by the part it was to play in the future counterculture. In the 1940s, the Libertarian Circle, in which Kenneth Rexroth played a major role, held meetings here. The Poets Follies between 1955 and 1958 brought poetry to the performance stage. Billed as "another session of San Francisco's unique Institution of Lower Learning," the final Follies featured a jazz band and Kenneth Rexroth, James Broughton, Michael Greig, Weldon Kees, Michael McClure, Vincent McHugh, Lawrence Ferlinghetti, and Lily Ayres, an exotic dancer who read the works of "Sarah Stripteasedale."

In April 1972, City Lights used Fugazi Hall to stage a City Lights Poets Theater benefit for Greek resistance to the new military regime. Writers from Greece joined Kay Boyle, Andrei Codrescu, Diane di Prima, Nanos Valaoritis, and Lawrence Ferlinghetti, who read his "Forty Odd Questions for the Greek Regime and One Cry for Freedom." "Where do we catch the boat for Plato's Republic?" the poem asks. Now Fugazi Hall is the permanent home of the long-running kitsch comedy revue, *Beach Blanket Babylon*. It babbles on brilliantly, year after year, much to the delight of tourists and assorted partygoers. In the fall of 2001, Beach Blanket generously lent its hall on a dark night to a sold-out reading by Ferlinghetti to benefit the San Francisco Poetry Center.

Return to the intersection of Columbus, Green, and Stockton. Here you can glance across the street at the ghost of the

Buon Gusto Market   21.
480 Columbus

In *Desolation Angels,* Jack Kerouac wrote about the wonderful food to be found at the Buon Gusto—"the hanging salamis and provolones and assortments of wine, and vegetable bins." In the 1950s the Buon Gusto stood here, one of many Italian grocers in the neighborhood—with fresh poultry, homemade Italian sausages, and handmade fresh pasta. If you walk a block up Columbus to Molinari's at 373 Columbus, you can catch the flavor of those tastes and smells.

Cross Columbus, walk north on Stockton, and you' ll soon pass

North Beach Restaurant / Rose Pistola 22.
1512 Stockton / 532 Columbus

In the mid-1980s Gregory Corso struck up a friendship with Lorenzo Petroni, proprietor of the North Beach. Corso stopped in for wine and conversation several times a week, but Petroni wouldn't let him drink without giving him something to eat first. In appreciation Corso made a painting for him based on Greek myths, using the restaurant's staff as models, and also wrote a poem for the restaurateur. One day they made a deal that if Corso quit smoking, Petroni would upgrade the wine they were drinking, but the next day they were back to the usual house wine. Corso said he was the only one singled out for special treatment at the North Beach Restaurant because his friends didn't deserve such good food, but he just wanted to keep a good thing to himself.

One of the finest restaurants in North Beach is Rose Pistola at 532 Columbus, with a side door on Stockton just across the street from the North Beach Restaurant. Its menu, featuring fresh fish and vegetables, somewhat resembles that of the famous Berkeley restaurant Chez Panisse. It wasn't around in the heyday of the Beats, but owner Reed Hearon appreciates neighborhood history and tradition. He named the place after Rose Pistola, a famously madcap hostess and restaurateur of the twenties and thirties, founder of the original Rose Pistola. On the back of the menu you'll read Lawrence Ferlinghetti's short poem, "A Recipe for Happiness in Khabarovsk or Anyplace:" "One grand boulevard with trees / with one grand café in sun / with strong black coffee in very small cups / One not necessarily very beautiful / man or woman who loves you / One fine day."

Go north on Stockton to the next corner of Union and turn right. Look for the street sign on the little dead-end alleyway around the corner.

Via Ferlinghetti 23.
Union east of Stockton

On April 24, 1994, through the forceful efforts of San Francisco supervisor Angela Alioto, the name of Price Row was changed to Via Ferlinghetti. It was unprecedented to name a street for a living person, but an exception to the rule for naming streets was made. At the dedication ceremony, Ferlinghetti's friends and neighbors gathered to hear tributes by Neeli Cherkovski, Diane di Prima, Anne Waldman, Philip Whalen, and others. "I testify that naming a street after Lawrence Ferlinghetti is not only an honor to Lawrence but a badge of respect and pride on the part of San Francisco," said Michael McClure. Ferlinghetti noted in his speech that in Prohibition days this alley had been where hearses and bootleggers parked, "a fitting place to be named for a poet." (This was not the last honor the city bestowed on Ferlinghetti: in October 1998 he was named the city's first Poet Laureate.)

Retrace your steps and stop midway along the park, facing 615 Union, where once there was the

New Riviera Hotel (now the Casa Melissa Retirement Home)   24.
615 Union

Bob Kaufman lived in the New Riviera in 1959 while editing *Beatitude* magazine. In those days the cheap hotel housed people down on their luck and living on the margins. Jack Hirschman also lived at the New Riviera from time to time after 1973. When he first came to North Beach he described the feeling: "The war had driven most everybody crazy to one degree or another. Lots of drinking, lots of loving, lots of poetry." A few years later, Jerry Kamstra used the New Riviera as one of the settings for his North Beach novel, *The Frisco Kid.*

Across the street is

Washington Square Park   25.
Stockton between Union and Filbert

Originally the site of a Mexican ranch owned by Juana Briones and later a cemetery, Washington Square is now the main public park in North Beach. It is the largest open space in the area and is usually filled with dogs, children, and sunbathers. In the early morning, it's inhabited by elderly Chinese people doing Chi Gong and Tai Chi. Richard Brautigan used a photo of himself posing in front of the statue of Ben Franklin (in the center of the park) on

RICHARD BRAUTIGAN IN WASHINGTON SQUARE.
BOOK COVER OF TROUT FISHING IN AMERICA

the cover of *Trout Fishing in America*. Some of the action in that book takes place in the park.

Philip Whalen remembers coaxing Jack Kerouac into the park one day to sit in the sun. Kerouac brought a gallon jug of Tokay wine and drank all too much as usual, despite Whalen's efforts to get him to slow down. This was the *Big Sur* period when Kerouac's drinking was tragically out of control. In that book he writes about "sitting in the park of the big Italian white church watching kids play and people go by."

On January 30, 1960, the *San Francisco Chronicle* reported on a gathering of 300 "beatniks" who had gathered in Washington Square protesting a series of marijuana busts. Jerry Kamstra, then a student, made a typical speech to protestors and a contingent of police: "I'm tired of being persecuted for not sharing the same social point of view as Officer Bigarani." The editor of the Beat newspaper *Underhound*, Chester Anderson, took the position that neighborhood problems stemmed not from a little pot smoking but from too many tourists, and he urged the locals to stop putting on a show for them.

Later in the 1960s the park was the location of poet

Daniel Moore's Floating Lotus Opera production of *Bliss Apocalypse*. City Lights (who had published Moore's *Dawn Visions* in 1964) sponsored this outdoor spectacle on a windy night in the square, to the amazed delight of the audience.

Ferlinghetti, who walks past the park every day on his way to the bookstore, has written several poems in which the park plays a part. "I Genitori Perduti" begins: "The dove-white gulls / on the wet lawn in Washington Square / in the early morning fog / each a little ghost in the gloaming . . ." Perhaps, if he were to rewrite the poem today, he would mention the noisy flock of parrots that have made the park its home. Allen Ginsberg wrote one of his last poems, "Ballad of the Skeletons," late one night while staying in the Washington Square Inn at the corner of Stockton and Filbert. Maybe the parrots kept him awake.

Directly across the park you'll see

Saints Peter and Paul Church 26.
666 Filbert

Looking like a big wedding cake, the Church of Saints Peter and Paul dominates the plaza. It's a little strange that a church should have drawn the number of the Antichrist, 666, as its address, but coincidences can be strange. This was the childhood parish of baseball player Joe DiMaggio and he and his new bride Marilyn Monroe were famously photographed on the steps here after their civil service wedding.

Ferlinghetti tells the story of how his dog Pooch went in to pay his respects to St. Rocco, who is always depicted with his faithful dog (see the little chapel just to the right of the main entrance). But a priest unceremoniously kicked Pooch out. And thereby hangs a tail. Years later, in a March 2002 issue of *Gourmet* magazine, Pooch got ghost-writer Ferlinghetti to castigate the priest in his name, satirically venting his resentment at having been given the boot by "a man in a long black dress." Perhaps he would have had better luck at the nearby Church of St. Francis of Assisi, the visionary who preached to the birds and spoke with a wolf. Ferlinghetti notes Sts. Peter and Paul in several poems, including the epic "The Old Italians Dying" and "A Report on a Happening in Washington Square San Francisco."

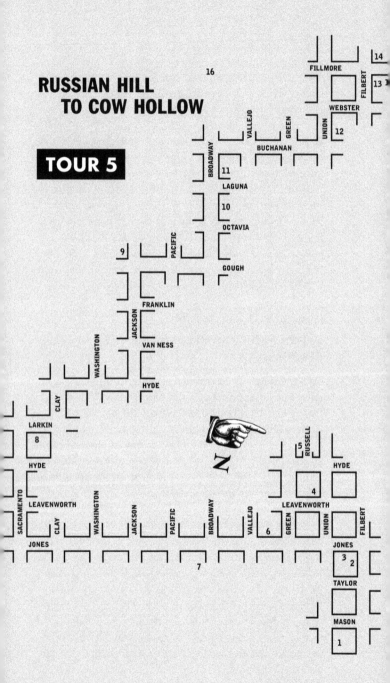

RUSSIAN HILL
TO COW HOLLOW

TOUR 5

16

FILLMORE

FILBERT

14

13

WEBSTER

VALLEJO

GREEN

UNION

12

BROADWAY

BUCHANAN

LAGUNA

11

OCTAVIA

10

PACIFIC

9

GOUGH

FRANKLIN

JACKSON

VAN NESS

WASHINGTON

HYDE

CLAY

LARKIN

8

HYDE

RUSSELL

5

HYDE

SACRAMENTO

LEAVENWORTH

LEAVENWORTH

4

LARKIN

CLAY

WASHINGTON

JACKSON

PACIFIC

BROADWAY

VALLEJO

GREEN

UNION

FILBERT

JONES

6

JONES

3

2

7

TAYLOR

MASON

1

CAROLYN CASSADY, JACK KEROUAC, AND CATHY CASSADY, 1952.
PHOTO BY NEAL CASSADY

RUSSIAN HILL AND COW HOLLOW
Russian Hill to the Marina District

Begin this tour a block west of Washington Square Park at

Intersection
(now the Evangelical Free Church) 1.
756 Union

This eye-catching building is still remembered as the site of an Intersection for the Arts' fabulous Tuesday night reading series in the sixties and seventies. In the late 1970s Intersection moved to the Mission district as North Beach began to lose its writers and artists because of higher and higher rents.

Continue up Union to the corner and turn right onto Mason for one block then left onto Filbert for almost two blocks to

David Meltzer's apartment 2.
973 Filbert

Poet David Meltzer was born into a musical family in Rochester, New York, and as a boy sang on the *Horn & Hardart Children's Hour* radio program. Later, he went to

BENEFIT FOR INTERSECTION POETRY SERIES
KENNETH REXROTH
TUESDAY JULY 2
~~JUNE 25~~
8:30 PM
756 UNION ST.
$1.50 Donation Requested

TO BE VIDEOTAPED BY ARRANGEMENT
WITH POETRY CENTER.

FLYER FOR INTERSECTION POETRY SERIES, 1974

school in Los Angeles, where he came into contact with the community that grew up around artists Wallace Berman and Bob Alexander. Meltzer moved on to San Francisco in 1957 when he was twenty, and he has lived in the Bay Area ever since. He was a regular performer at The Cellar's poetry and jazz nights; with his combination of literary and musical talent, this milieu was perfect for him. In the late 1950s, when painter Joan Brown gave up her place on the ground floor of this apartment building, David and his wife Tina moved in. Since their small pad was behind a garage, the apartment filled with suffocating exhaust fumes whenever a car started. So after two years they moved to something safer just up the hill. Meltzer's first book of poetry, *Ragas,* was published while he was living here. One poem, "Filbert Street," refers to a "white-haired, fat Italian mamma with mustache" whom he always saw sitting at a third-floor window on Filbert.

Continue to the corner of Jones and turn left uphill. In the middle of the block on the left side is

David Meltzer's apartment   3.
2026 Jones

It's a steep climb to David and Tina Meltzer's next apartment, which they took over from a friend who danced flamenco at the Spaghetti Factory. The Meltzers lived here for ten years until they moved to Mill Valley at the end of the sixties. Their three baby girls were all born in the living room of this apartment. Poet John Wieners was an occasional, if atypical, baby sitter. Meltzer recalls coming home late one night to find Wieners sitting in the dark kitchen with a candle lit, cigarette ashes overflowing the ashtray, listening over and over to the classic Billie Holiday recording of "Strange Fruit," as the children slept soundly in their beds.

Continue up Jones to Union and turn right uphill to the corner of Leavenworth.

DAVID MELTZER PERFORMING AT THE CELLAR. PHOTO BY C.R. SNYDER

DAVID AND TINA MELTZER AT THE CELLAR.   PHOTO BY C.R. SNYDER

Claude Pélieu and Mary Beach's flat 4.
1955 Leavenworth

Claude Pélieu and Mary Beach lived in the building on the southwest corner of this intersection during the 1960s. Pélieu was an expatriate from Gaullist France; together he and his wife, Mary Beach, an American painter and writer, collaborated on translations of many Beat writers for the French publisher Christian Bourgois. They published nearly all of Allen Ginsberg's poetry and also important work by Burroughs and Ferlinghetti. Beach and Pélieu's translations of Bob Kaufman brought him widespread fame in France. When Kaufman's wife Eileen salvaged bits and pieces of his poetry from dozens of paper scraps, Pélieu and Beach helped her assemble them for *Golden Sardine,* published by City Lights in the Pocket Poets Series. While living here, they also published Beach Books Texts & Documents, including far-out works by Burroughs, Ginsberg, and Carl Solomon (to whom "Howl" was dedicated). After the sixties, they returned to France, where Pélieu took part in spontaneous Happenings and was a mover in the Fluxus movement and Beach continued a career as a painter.

Go west on Union one more block to Hyde. Turn left and look for Russell Street, on the right about halfway down the block. Turn right and stop at

Neal and Carolyn Cassady's house   5.
29 Russell

One of the most significant Beat sites in the city is this little gabled house, on this little street on Russian Hill. Neal and Carolyn Cassady moved into this bungalow in 1949 with their infant daughter Cathy, and it was here that Neal began an autobiography, part of which was eventually published posthumously as *The First Third* by City Lights. Neal found a job at a Firestone tire shop near Van Ness and Carolyn worked at a doctor's office near Union Square during this period. Neal invited Jack Kerouac to come to San Francisco to teach him how to write, but Jack's visit didn't last long. Carolyn kicked both Neal and Jack out of the house after a riotous escapade with their old buddy Henri Cru. One of their Denver friends, Helen Hinkle, moved in with Carolyn to help with the baby.

PHOTO BY BILL MORGAN

CASSADY HOUSE ON RUSSELL STREET TODAY.

JACK KEROUAC, 1953.

Meanwhile, Diane Hansen was about to give birth to Neal's son and, although he was already married to Carolyn, he decided to go back East to marry Diane. (In those days to be an "illegitimate" child was still a social stigma and Neal wanted to do the right thing.) However, a few days after the wedding with Diane, Neal drove back to San Francisco because he wanted to be with Carolyn. For a while he thought he might be able to juggle two families, one on each coast, but this proved impossible, so he moved back to Russell Street in mid-October 1950, and in September 1951, Carolyn gave birth to John Allen Cassady, named for Neal's two best friends, John (Jack) Kerouac and Allen Ginsberg.

In January 1952, Kerouac traveled cross-country again and arrived at the Russell Street house late one night. Kerouac wrote, "He [Neal] came to the door stark naked and it might have been the President knocking for all he cared. He received the world in the raw." Kerouac was to stay in their attic for the next six months, writing and rewriting several of his big books, including *On the Road, Doctor Sax,* and *Visions of Cody.* One night when Kerouac was walking around Russian Hill he happened upon a film crew making *Sudden Fear* with Joan Crawford. He turned the episode into a short story, "Joan Rawshanks in the Fog," which found its way into *Visions of Cody.* The stairs to the attic went through the Cassadys' bedroom, and Kerouac was so shy that he stayed in the attic for hours on end rather than disturb the couple. The attic was only half-finished, and Kerouac typed on a desk made from a three- by four-foot sheet of plywood. There was a bed on the floor and a typewriter, paper, Dexedrine, a radio, bongo drums, and a tape recorder for the new spontaneous prose style he was developing. Kerouac's technique was inspired by the flow of Cassady's nonstop monologues.

When Neal went back to work on the railroad, he encouraged Carolyn and Jack to become lovers. At first they thought he was kidding, but later they took up his suggestion. For a few months it seemed a perfect three-way relationship, but everything fell apart one night when Neal and Jack tried to smuggle another woman into the attic. Carolyn kicked them both out again, and then made strict rules before Neal could return. In August 1952 she and Neal moved to a house in San Jose. The entire complex relationship is described in Carolyn's memoir *Off the Road*.

Return to Hyde Street and turn right to the next street, which is Green. Turn left and go up the hill two blocks to Jones Street. Turn right on Jones and stop at

NEAL CASSADY AT THE WHEEL, WITH ANNE MURPHY.   PHOTO © ALLEN GINSBERG TRUST

Donald M. Allen's apartment 6.
1815 Jones (between Green and Vallejo)

Before he left Grove Press in New York, Don Allen completed editing *The New American Poetry, 1945–1960,* the definitive anthology of the era. In 1960 he moved to San Francisco and in 1962 found a small apartment here, where he lived until 1972, when he and many others left the city for the village of Bolinas, up the coast. Of his Jones Street home he wrote, "There I edited and published three titles by Richard Brautigan: *Trout Fishing in America, In Watermelon Sugar* and *The Pill Versus the Springhill Mine Disaster.* And there I entertained many friends: Robin Blaser, Robert Creeley, Robert Duncan, Allen Ginsberg, Bobbie Louise Hawkins, Joanne Kyger, Philip Lamantia, Anne Rice BV [before vampires], and Gary Snyder. Charles Olson stayed with me for a month in 1962 and one evening Ed Sanders, then touring with the Fugs, and Janice Joplin joined Olson and me for drinks. Janice brought her own bottle of Southern Comfort. Charles was wearing a small pigtail. We went to the then-excellent Four Seas restaurant [on Grant Avenue] in Chinatown for dinner."

Continue south on Jones for two more blocks to Broadway. Turn left and stop where Broadway begins to descend toward North Beach again. There is a cozy little bench on the downhill side of the wall, in case you'd like to rest your dogs.

Herbert Gold's place 7.
Broadway east of Jones

Novelist and essayist Herbert Gold has lived on Russian Hill for the past forty years. On the brink of the hill, his place has a spectacular view of North Beach, and Herb has a steep climb home from the restaurants, bookstores, and coffee shops he loves. Gold was a classmate of Allen Ginsberg at Columbia University in the 1940s, and they both wrote for the campus literary magazine there. Once when Gold and Ginsberg were walking down Russian Hill to North Beach, they heard what sounded like a mimeograph machine, and Allen stopped, listened a moment, and exclaimed, "A poet!" Of course.

Among the many books Gold wrote here, *Bohemia:*

Where Art, Angst, Love, and Strong Coffee Meet and *Travels in San Francisco* touch on Gold's associations with the Beats.

Return to Jones Street and turn left, walk five blocks south to Sacramento, then turn right on Sacramento and continue three blocks to Larkin. Turn right again and stop at

David Meltzer's apartment 8.
1514 Larkin

Living in Los Angeles in 1957, David Meltzer was discovering that it was not a poet's town. He drove to San Francisco with artist Wallace Berman, who was coming up for a weekend, and then David stayed on and took a job in a book warehouse. His first apartment was really just part of a room, here at 1514 Larkin, which he shared with Norman Rose, who got him his warehouse job. The room had been an old radio repair shop with a display window covered by paper to afford privacy. It was all very Spartan: Meltzer slept in the window alcove and Rose slept on a cot. Meltzer often went with Michael McClure to Joe Dunn's apartment on Nob Hill for Dunn's weekly literary gathering. The two were a little younger than the other poets at these soirées and had different sensibilities. Robert Duncan took to McClure but was always cold to Meltzer. According to McClure, the poems by Dunn's Black Mountain friends were beautiful but very difficult to understand. Meltzer's poems, on the other hand, were both beautiful and completely understandable, and this offended Duncan and company.

Continue on Larkin to the corner of Clay. Turn left at Clay then right on Polk. Walk north two blocks to Jackson Street, then turn left, walk three blocks, crossing Van Ness. On the left, at Gough, you will find

Lawrence Ferlinghetti's first residence in San Francisco 9.
1901 Jackson

In 1951 the building at 1901 Jackson was a Guest House, (a uniquely San Franciscan genre of rooming house). Today it has been renovated as one of the grand mansions

PHOTO BY BILL MORGAN

on the slopes of Pacific Heights. When Ferlinghetti arrived in San Francisco after finishing his doctorate at the Sorbonne, he looked in the yellow pages and picked a Guest House called the Chateau Bleu because he assumed (incorrectly) that people there would speak French. At the time, he was writing a novel and found a job teaching French in an adult education program. That year he went back east to Florida and married his sweetheart, Selden Kirby-Smith, whom everyone called Kirby. When they returned to San Francisco, they found an apartment on Divisidero Street.

Turn right down the hill on Gough for two blocks to Broadway and turn left for two more blocks to the northeast corner of Laguna.

Peter Lambert DuPeru's place   10.
1998 Broadway

The Broadway Laguna Residence Club, which once stood here, was where Peter DuPeru lived in 1954. In *Desolation Angels* Jack Kerouac described DuPeru (under the name of Richard de Chili), "who wanders around Frisco at night in long fast strides, all alone, examining the examples of architecture, strange hodgepodge notions and bay windows and garden walls, giggling, alone in the night . . ." Allen Ginsberg was drawn to hustlers like DuPeru, Herbert Huncke, and Bill Garver, who were his guides to the subterranean world of homosexuals, pimps, petty criminals, and addicts. Ginsberg was a well-educated college boy and not always welcome in this milieu without a friend on the inside. In his *Journals Mid-Fifties* he describes DuPeru as "a certain kind of archetypal bohemian" and used a page and a half to list the contents of DuPeru's small overnight bag: ". . . a white & black box of Smith's Cough Drops—1/4 loaf of bread—Miracle Whip Salad Dressing—Fungi Rex Powder (athlete's foot) —Book—*La Société Française au Dix-Septième Siècle . . .*" Even Allen had problems with his lowlife friends, though, and after DuPeru trashed Ginsberg's hotel room for no apparent reason, Allen was too frightened to let him stay any longer.

Continue west on Broadway into the next block and stop at the modern apartment building on your right.

American Academy of Asian Studies   11.
2030 Broadway

The American Academy of Asian Studies stood here when Alan Watts was director. It's gone now, replaced by the current ugly structure, but the importance of Watts and his academy to the Beats cannot be overlooked. Watts played a seminal role in popularizing Buddhism in America and many Beat writers got their first exposure to Buddhism through his books. Financial difficulties forced Watts to resign in 1956 and the academy closed the following year. Watts attracted a diverse assortment of students and faculty, including both Michael Murphy and Richard Price, who went on to found the Esalen Institute at Big Sur.

Gary Snyder had a friendship with Watts since his early days at Berkeley, when Gary studied meditation at the Buddhist Church there. Jack Kerouac, Allen Ginsberg, and Peter Orlovsky came to the academy to hear him lecture. His knowledge of Eastern philosophy attracted other writers—James Broughton, Diane di Prima, Joanne Kyger, and Philip Whalen—who transmitted their interest in Buddhism to the next literary generation.

In *Desolation Angels,* Kerouac described in detail a visit to Watts that he and Peter Orlovsky once made, walking "up Broadway hill among flowers and fresh air," and the mischief they made as they looked for him. Kerouac's pseudonym for Watts was Alex Aums. In 1973, Watts died at the age of fifty-eight and was cremated, his ashes buried in a stupa on the slopes of Mount Tamalpais.

Turn right at the next corner onto Buchanan and walk three blocks downhill to Union. Turn left and stop midway on the north side of the block.

Kenneth Rexroth Books 12.
2038 Union (second floor)

In the late 1960s Kenneth Rexroth decided to make a little money by selling some of the thousands of books he had collected over the years, including the many review copies he continually received. At that time, Rexroth's friend Horace Schwartz, who had a small press called Goad, wanted to run a bookstore and asked if he could name it after Rexroth. Even though Rexroth supplied most of the stock, he owned no part of Kenneth Rexroth Books. The store didn't last long, in part because the stock wasn't consistent, even though Schwartz compared himself to the giant Strand Bookstore in New York City in his advertising.

Paul Bowles visited this store when he was in San Francisco and Ira Gershwin came by once: both were disappointed to find that Rexroth didn't run the store. Schwartz tried to sell Bowles a copy of a Rexroth book for $2, but Bowles accused him of price gouging.

Turn right at the next corner and proceed along Webster for one block before turning left on Filbert. Stop near the corner of Fillmore, on the north side, where 2192 once stood (it's now a small parking lot).

Spatsa Gallery 13.
2192 Filbert

In the 1950s, this part of Cow Hollow was a backwater of unwanted buildings and small-service businesses such as garages and repair shops. The low rents made it a perfect site for a new gallery scene. After the Six Gallery closed, California School of Fine Arts student Dimitri Grachis paid $35 a month for the Spatsa Gallery space here, a gallery he named for the Greek island where his father was born. From 1958 until 1962 Spatsa showed Bruce Conner, William Morris, and other rising young artists. Nearby were the East-West, John Gilmore, and Green Galleries.

Across Fillmore and a little to the north you'll see

PHOTO BY BILL MORGAN

Six Gallery 14.
3119 Fillmore

In San Francisco's postwar literary history, one event stands taller than all the others, Allen Ginsberg's 1955 public reading of "Howl" at the Six Gallery. A bronze plaque commemorating the reading was placed in front of the building in 2005. In 1952 Robert Duncan, his partner the collagist Jess Collins, and Harry Jacobus rented an old auto repair garage at this address, for which they paid $50 a month and created the King Ubu Gallery, which flourished a little over a year. They showed contemporary underground art, coupled with an alternative space for music, plays, and poetry readings. It was at the King Ubu that Robert Duncan, at the end of his play *Faust Foutu,* took off all his clothes to explain nakedness to the audience. Years later, when Ginsberg did the same thing in Los Angeles, people thought it outrageously daring and it became one of the most famous Ginsberg stories.

On October 31, 1954, nine months after King Ubu closed, six artists opened a new gallery, which they called the Six Gallery. The founding six were Wallace Hedrick, Hayward King, Deborah Remington, John Allen Ryan, David Simpson, and Jack Spicer. On opening day they displayed a toilet in the front window with a draft notice suspended over it. During the McCarthy era and the Korean War, this was a daring gesture, and the police showed up immediately, forcing them to remove the installation.

Until 1957 the Six Gallery continued to host unorthodox exhibitions, readings, and performances.

The night of October 7, 1955, was a defining moment in American literature and consciousness. A few poets who had not known one another very long gathered to read to a crowd of around 100 people. Kenneth Rexroth acted as master of ceremonies, introducing Michael McClure, Gary Snyder, Philip Whalen, Philip Lamantia, and Allen Ginsberg. Jack Kerouac was present but was too shy to read. He shouted encouragement and collected money for jug wine to pass around. The crowd got into the swing of things and by the time Ginsberg got up to read "Howl" it was wild. As Ginsberg himself not so modestly reviewed the performance: "The reading was delivered by the poet, rather surprised at his own power, drunk on the platform, becoming increasingly sober as he read, driving forward with a strange ecstatic intensity, delivering a spiritual confession to an astounded audience—ending in tears which had restored to American poetry the prophetic consciousness it had lost since the conclusion of Hart Crane's *The Bridge*." Lawrence Ferlinghetti was in the audience. He went home and sent a telegram to Ginsberg asking to publish "Howl." Ginsberg's may have been the most spectacular poem, but it was not the only impressive poetry read that night, for each of the six poets spoke poems that helped establish the Beat Movement as a revolutionary force.

Across Fillmore and a little farther north is

The Matrix 15.
3138 Fillmore

On September 13, 1965, a new group called Jefferson Airplane debuted at the Matrix nightclub and created a sensation. As one of the headquarters for the new San Francisco sound, The Matrix later hosted many other groups like Big Brother and the Holding Company, Quicksilver Messenger Service, the Grateful Dead, Sopwith Camel, Country Joe and the Fish, the Doors, Youngbloods, Hot Tuna, New Riders of the Purple Sage, and Johnny Winter.

If you have the energy for a long hike, return to Union, turn right and walk four blocks to Divisidero, then turn left and go five blocks, just past Jackson on the east side to

Lawrence Ferlinghetti's garret   16.
2324 Divisidero

On April 10, 1951, Ferlinghetti married Selden Kirby-Smith and the couple rented a three-room apartment on the top floor of 2324 Divisidero. Kirby found a job teaching at the Catherine Branson School, and Lawrence taught a course in modern American literature at the San Francisco Institute of Music and Art a block and a half away, for a few dollars a week. (He taught mostly Thoreau's *Walden*.) Kirby had gone to Swarthmore with Holly Beye, and through her and her husband David Ruff, the Ferlinghettis met Kenneth Rexroth and Kenneth Patchen. The newlyweds lived here for a while before moving to Chestnut Street in North Beach.

PHOTO BY BILL MORGAN

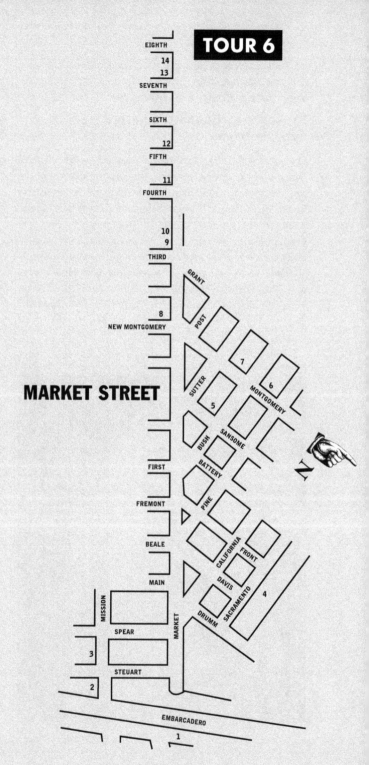

TOUR 6

EIGHTH
14
13
SEVENTH

SIXTH
12
FIFTH
11
FOURTH

10
9
THIRD

GRANT
8
POST
NEW MONTGOMERY

7
SUTTER
MONTGOMERY
6
5
MARKET STREET
BUSH
SANSOME
BATTERY
FIRST
PINE
FREMONT

BEALE
CALIFORNIA
FRONT
MAIN
DAVIS
SACRAMENTO
4
MISSION
DRUMM
SPEAR
MARKET
3
STEUART
2

EMBARCADERO
1

N

LawRENCE FERLINGHETTI AT HIS PAINTING STUDIO IN THE AUDIFFRED BUILDING, CA.1957.
PHOTO BY HARRY REDL

MARKET STREET:
The Embarcadero, Financial District, Market Street to Civic Center

Market Street and The Embarcadero

Radical urban development has so completely changed The Embarcadero and Market Street that retracing the footsteps of the Beat Generation through this neighborhood is difficult to do. The atmosphere of this area when the city was a thriving port city in the forties and fifties is gone, along with many of the bus stations, cafeterias, and

SAN FRANCISCO FERRY BUILDING.   PHOTO BY BILL MORGAN

movie houses that figured in life on the road. Along The Embarcadero were the docks and small businesses that supplied ships and seamen, which have all relocated across the bay along with the working port.

Market Street, or The Slot as it was called, cuts a diagonal from the Ferry Terminal to the west, up the hills away from the waterfront as Kerouac describes in *Lonesome Traveler.*

Begin at the foot of Market Street in the plaza in front of the

Ferry Building   1.
The Embarcadero at Market

One of the few landmarks that survived the great earthquake of 1906 is the stately Ferry Building on The Embarcadero. When the ferries stopped crossing the bay in 1958, the building was converted into offices facing inward toward the city. Now the building has been restored to look out once again on the great harbor. Before the Bay Bridge was built most people coming to San Francisco arrived via ferry with upward of 170 boats a day docking here. As one of the most famous buildings in the city it has also found its way into many literary works. In his poem "Thru the Vortex West Coast to East," Ginsberg invokes the "Ferry building's sweet green clock lamps black Embarcadero waters . . ." as he heads east.

On January 5, 1951, when Lawrence Ferlinghetti arrived in San Francisco for the first time, he came by rail to Oakland and then by ferry across the bay. He remembers feeling like Ishmael in *Moby-Dick* landing on a distant shore, and he recorded his impressions in the third person years later: "Approaching the Ferry Building, he stood on deck and saw a small shining white city, looking rather like Tunis seen from Seaward, a Mediterranean city, with small white houses on hillsides, brilliant in January sunshine . . . It seemed an early morning city, rising up the hills, the air itself flashing with sunlight—that special San Francisco January light, so different from the pearly light of Paris beloved by painters. He was the first off the ferry, with no idea where to go, except up. The city rose up before him as he started up Market Street, his sea bag over his shoulder, paintbox under arm, still wearing his Basque beret. He walked and walked and walked that day, and got the impression that the natives had a kind of *island mentality,* considering themselves San Franciscans first, on an island which wasn't necessarily a part of the United States."

Ferlinghetti thought he'd like a fishing job, but since he couldn't speak Sicilian he couldn't communicate with the fishermen. Then he considered teaching at the Maritime Academy. He wanted to join the union, but he couldn't join the union because he didn't have a seaman's job and couldn't get a seaman's job because he didn't belong to the union, even though he'd been a commanding officer on a navy ship in World War II and was a qualified navigator.

As you face the Ferry Building with your back to Market Street, on your right two blocks south is a building at the corner of Mission and The Embarcadero.

Audiffred Building   2.
1–21 Mission

The brick Audiffred Building with the gray mansard roof and white trim was built in 1889 by Hippolite D'Audiffred, and for a time it housed the boisterous Bulkhead Saloon. During the 1906 earthquake, fire threatened the entire city. Soldiers were deployed to destroy hundreds of buildings to create firebreaks. They were ordered to blow up the Audiffred, which stood directly in their path; but the Bulkhead's bartender had other plans. He offered each soldier a keg of whiskey to spare the building, and it is still standing today. In the late 1970s a fire finally did gut the Audiffred, but the owners restored and beautified it.

There were artists' lofts here for many years. In the early fifties Ferlinghetti moved into the loft vacated by the Abstract Expressionist artist Hassel Smith. It cost $29 a month. A pot bellied stove provided heat and there was no electricity above the ground floor. Artists Elmer Bischoff, Howard Hack, Frank Lobdell, and Martin Snipper also had studios in the building at one time or another.

In 1955, Ginsberg and Kerouac arrived at the Key System Bus Terminal on the corner of First and Mission and ran into poets Gary Snyder and Philip Whalen by chance. During their conversation they decided it would be a fine idea to ask Michael McClure and Philip Lamantia to join them in a reading that would be called "Six Poets at the Six Gallery." That reading would revitalize twentieth-century poetry.

Walk along Mission Street away from The Embarcadero, crossing Steuart. Stop at the old post office building, which takes up the south side of the entire block.

U.S. Post Office, Rincon Annex 3.
180 Steuart

Peter Orlovsky worked at this post office branch, driving a mail truck in 1955 when he first met Allen Ginsberg. Ginsberg refers to those days in his "Continuation of a Long Poem of These States." This post office building is worth visiting to see the Anton Refregier murals in the lobby. These twenty-seven paintings, a WPA project, created a stir when they were painted in 1948. By 1953, as McCarthyism heated up, right-wingers wanted them destroyed. Offensive images included Sir Francis Drake with his hand on the entire globe, Russian explorers and Communist flags, and scenes from the infamous Tom Mooney case. (Mooney had been falsely charged with a 1917 bombing that took place only a block away from this building at Steuart and Market.) Ferlinghetti, who was writing art criticism back then, reported on the unsuccessful attempts to rid the city of the subversive paintings and his piece in the New York–based *Arts Digest* helped save the murals from destruction.

Exit the post office and walk north on Spear one block to Market Street. Turn left and stop between Main and Beale about a block and a half to the west. From Beale Street you can look north on Davis Street two blocks to the modern buildings of the Embarcadero Center toward the site of the

National Union of Marine Cooks   4.
86 Commercial Street (now gone)

There is no use walking down Davis to Commercial looking for number 86, because even the street on which this union hall stood is gone. It has all been replaced by high-rise commercial development. This was the location of the Marine Cooks and Stewards Union Hall, where Kerouac, hoping to catch a ship, met Charley Mew and Al Sublette, a black hipster who introduced him to the Frisco jazz scene. Sublette took part in the conversations with Cassady that Kerouac was taping while living in the Cassadys' attic on Russell Street in 1952. Those conversations formed the nucleus for the book, *Visions of Cody*. Despite many attempts, Kerouac shipped out only once from the port of San Francisco. That time he took a job on a

ship that went through the Panama Canal, but when he got to New Orleans, he jumped ship without completing his assignment.

Cross Market Street at Fremont and continue west along Bush Street to Sansome. Pause at the large building on the southwest corner; above the main entrance archway is a medallion emblazoned with an oil derrick.

JACK KEROUAC AND NEAL CASSADY. PHOTO BY CAROLYN CASSADY

Standard Oil Building 5.
225 Bush

In his *Book of Blues* Jack Kerouac describes the Standard Oil Building with its huge, red, neon Pegasus on the roof. That sign is now gone, but in the past it served as a beacon to let you know you were coming into the great city as you crossed the bay from Oakland. Kerouac mentions the sign in both *Desolation Angels* and in a short poem in *Book of Blues*. "Here in the Standard / Building / Flying High / the / Riding Horse / A Red."

Continue one more block up Bush to Montgomery. On the northwest corner is the block-long Russ Building.

Foster's Cafeteria (now gone) 6.
235 Montgomery

Foster's Cafeterias were a popular, pre-McDonald's chain of cheap restaurants during the 1950s—neon-lit, Formica-tabled, open all night, and a favorite Beat hangout. The one that was here was where Allen Ginsberg and Peter Orlovsky exchanged marriage vows in 1955, after talking into the wee hours of the morning "trying to figure out what we were going to do, who we were to each other, and what we wanted out of each other," as Ginsberg later wrote. They were to remain companions for the next forty-two years until Ginsberg's death in 1997. Orlovsky was with him when he died.

Turn and walk south on Montgomery to the middle of the next block. The Schwab Building now occupies the site of 127 Montgomery, which was close to the old Alexander Building still on the southwest corner of Bush.

Towne-Oller Associates 7.
127 Montgomery

When Ginsberg came to San Francisco in 1954 he tried unsuccessfully to land a job on a newspaper. Because of his earlier New York experience in market research, he found work doing "marketing studies of toiletries on the front counters of supermarkets, correlating them with money spent on advertising campaigns by toothpaste companies or Johnson & Johnson baby powder and baby oil" as he put it in his *Journals Mid-Fifties*. Ginsberg's job paid him a handsome salary of $450 a month, and he had his own office and a secretary. Later he considered it "the best job I'd had in the regular commercial wheel." But he couldn't stand it for very long, and quit in May 1955 to follow the life of a poet.

Continue south on Montgomery to Market Street. Directly in front of you on the southwest corner of Market and New Montgomery is the Palace Hotel. Look for the discreet sign and go inside to see their magnificent lobby.

Palace Hotel 8.
633–665 Market

The opulent Palace Hotel was not the kind of place Beat writers could afford, however, it was the site of the first political demonstration that Allen Ginsberg ever joined. Before the 1960s he had rarely been motivated by political issues, but he joined pickets here, on October 28, 1963, who were protesting the visit of Madame Nhu, the wife of Vietnam's secret-police chief and sister-in-law of President Diem. Ginsberg carried a handmade placard on which he'd written a protest poem for the occasion. The demonstration drew 500 marchers and was the largest to greet Madame Nhu on her U.S. visit. This was the first of countless protests Ginsberg would make over the next ten years against American involvement in Vietnam.

Continue west on Market and stop in front of 717 Market, just a few buildings past the corner of Third Street.

Federal Writers' Project 9.
717 Market

The Federal Writers' Project, one of the divisions of the WPA, had offices here during the depression. There is still a bit of art deco ornamentation around the windows of the upper floors, but otherwise the building's detail work has been erased through recent modernizations. Kenneth Rexroth was on the editorial staff of the project's American Guide Series, preparing the California state guide and a guide to the city of San Francisco. One of his coworkers was poet and painter Madeline Gleason, later the founder of the San Francisco Poetry Guild.

Nearby at 721 Market you'll see the site of one of the many

Market Street Movies 10.

Everyone went to the movies in the pretelevision forties and fifties, and the largest concentration of movie theaters in San Francisco was along Market Street. Jack Kerouac loved to watch monster movies, and he describes going to one with Gregory Corso in *Desolation Angels*. "First we dig the pictures on the wall. 'It's a nowhere picture, we can't go see it,' says [Corso]. 'There's no monsters, all it

NEAL CASSADY AND NATALIE JACKSON UNDER THE MARQUEE AT 721 MARKET STREET, 1955.
PHOTO © ALLEN GINSBERG TRUST

is a moonman with a suit on, I wanta see monstrous dinosaurs and mammals of the other worlds. Who wants to pay fifty cents to see guys with machines and panels.'" While walking with Ginsberg along Market Street, Neal Cassady and his girlfriend Natalie Jackson stopped under the theater marquee of the Marlon Brando flick, *The Wild One,* long enough for Ginsberg to snap their picture. Ginsberg captioned the photo as "Cassady conscious of his role in eternity," and it has become one of Ginsberg's most famous photographs. The old theater building is slated for renovation or demolition.

Walk one more block west along Market and stop after crossing Fourth Street in front of the Old Navy Store, at the

Brotherhood of Railroad Trainmen   11.
821 Market

The Pacific Building, built in 1907, might remind you of Louis Sullivan's Carson Pirie Scott store in Chicago, which was used as the model. This is where the offices of the Brotherhood of Railroad Trainmen were in the 1940s. Both Neal Cassady and Jack Kerouac were members of that union when they worked for the Southern Pacific. When

Cassady injured his leg, the union took over his case against the railroad. The final settlement took two long years, but finally Cassady was awarded enough compensation to buy a modest house in Los Gatos.

Continue west along Market Street and stop in front of

Vic Tanney Gym   12.
949 Market

This building housed the Vic Tanney Gym in the 1950s. When Michael McClure first arrived in San Francisco he found a job here. He recalls, "I worked six days a week, 12 hours a day, managing Tanney's but it was a strange scene with wrestlers, and street thieves, weight heads, wandering loonies, and those ambitious to help their bodies." The long hours on the job also afforded him plenty of time to work out and write poetry. While working in the gym he met many memorable characters, including one instructor who had sung scat with Kerouac a decade earlier.

Continue along Market Street and stop at the corner of Seventh Street.

Bus Stations   13.

The old bus stations of America have nearly all disappeared. Now, if bus stations exist at all, they are mostly small ticket booths in large parking lots on city outskirts, but in the days of the Beats, the bus station was a transportation hub, an essential fact of life providing a cheap way to get from coast to coast. In San Francisco, each bus line had its own terminal. Greyhound was near this corner, Continental Trailways was at 75 Fifth Street, and the Gray Line was at 425 Fourth Street. All these terminals are gone, victims of progress. In his books, Jack Kerouac cites them all. In *On the Road,* Kerouac slept while riding the bus across the Oakland Bay Bridge, and so he saw San Francisco for the first time as he stepped out of the Fourth Street bus station. From this description we can be certain that he took the Gray Line. In *Desolation Angels* he arrived at the Seventh Street terminal from Seattle, where he describes conversation with the black baggage handlers. This had to have been the Greyhound.

When Ginsberg couldn't get a railroad job, even with Cassady's recommendation, he worked for Greyhound instead. In 1956 he wrote in his journal "I had lost my poetry mind for several weeks working in the Greyhound terminal under the stairs in the basement." He used the experience to write one of his best early poems, "In the Baggage Room at Greyhound," which begins "In the depths of the Greyhound Terminal / sitting dumbly on a baggage truck looking at the sky waiting for the Los Angeles Express to depart / worrying about eternity over the Post Office roof in the night-time red downtown heaven . . ." Coincidentally, poet Ed Dorn worked in the same baggage room at the same time as Ginsberg, but on a different shift.

Continue one more block west along Market Street and stop just before Eighth Street in front of the Trinity Plaza apartments.

Crystal Palace Market   14.
1175 Market

Gary Snyder was a hardy outdoorsman who spent his summers mountain climbing, maintaining forest trails, and working on fire crews and at fire lookouts. On several occasions he helped get fire spotter jobs in the North Cascades for Kerouac and Whalen, where they'd have plenty of time for uninterrupted writing. The Army Navy surplus store on Market Street was a fine source of tough used gear and clothing for this type of activity.

Snyder also liked to shop at the Crystal Palace Market, once a large Asian grocery at this location. In the 1950s, Jack Kerouac described getting provisions in the *Dharma Bums*. "Now as for food, I went down to Market Street to the Crystal Palace market and bought my favorite dry cereal, bulgur, which is a kind of a Bulgarian cracked rough wheat and I'm going to stick pieces of bacon in it, little square chunks, that'll make a fine supper for all three of us."

TOUR 7

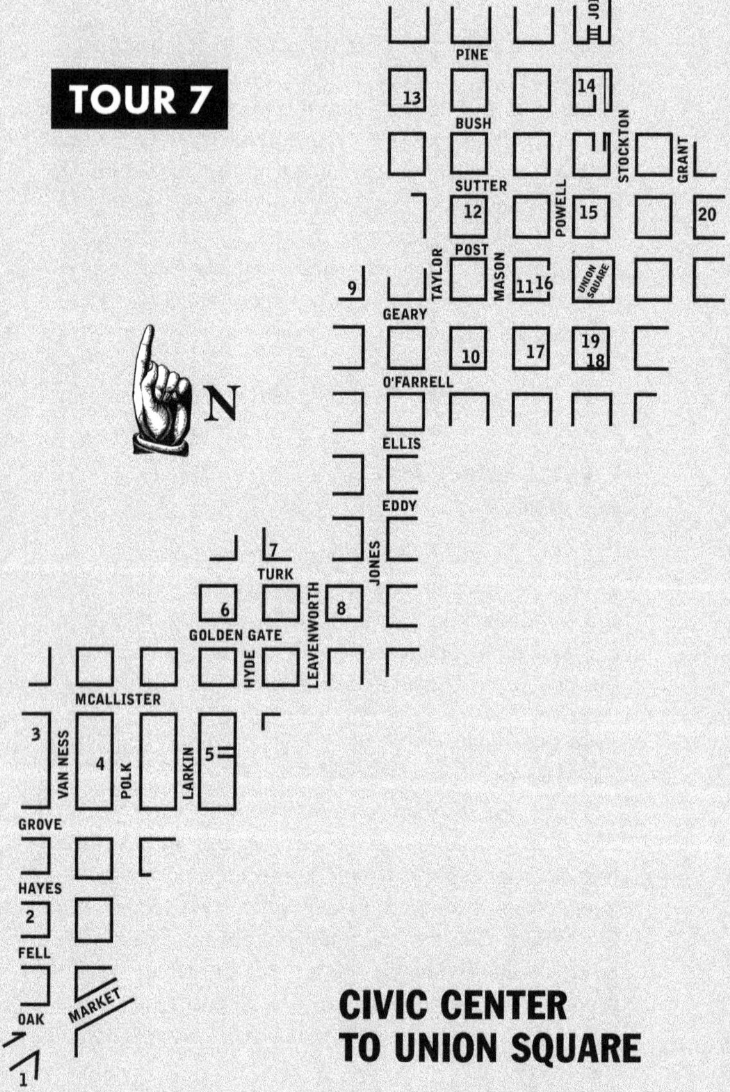

CIVIC CENTER
TO UNION SQUARE

Streets labeled on map:
JOICE, PINE, BUSH, SUTTER, STOCKTON, GRANT, POWELL, POST, TAYLOR, MASON, UNION SQUARE, GEARY, O'FARRELL, ELLIS, EDDY, JONES, TURK, LEAVENWORTH, GOLDEN GATE, HYDE, LARKIN, MCALLISTER, POLK, VAN NESS, GROVE, HAYES, FELL, OAK, MARKET

N

ALLEN GINSBERG 'S VISION OF "MOLOCH" IN THE SIR FRANCIS DRAKE HOTEL.
PHOTO BY HARRY REDL

CIVIC CENTER TO UNION SQUARE

Begin this tour on the southwest corner of Market and Van Ness in front of the Honda dealership.

Fillmore West   1.
Market and Van Ness

In many ways the San Francisco sound in rock grew out of the groundwork laid down by the freewheeling Beat culture. In 1968 Ron Rakow of the Grateful Dead formed a partnership with Jefferson Airplane and Quicksilver Messenger Service to bring such musicians as Thelonious Monk, Dr. John, and the Charlatans to this auditorium, at the time called the Carousel. Six months later, rock impresario Bill Graham moved his operation from the Fillmore Auditorium (at Fillmore and Geary) to this hall, which he renamed Fillmore West. From 1968 until it closed in 1971, Fillmore West presented Janice Joplin, Big Brother and the Holding Company, the Who, Mike Bloomfield, Ray Charles, Eric Clapton, Creedence Clearwater, Aretha Franklin, Al Kooper, Carlos Santana, Taj Mahal, Van Morrison, Johnny Winter, and many, many others.

Walk north on Van Ness for two blocks, turn left onto Hayes. On the left side of the street is the

Nourse Auditorium   2.
275 Hayes

For months in 1968, David Meltzer had been organizing "The Incredible Poetry Reading," which happened to be booked here at the Nourse Auditorium on the same day as Robert Kennedy's funeral. Although the mood was dark, as if the killing foreshadowed the end of utopian dreams, the show went on. Ferlinghetti read a poem he wrote specifically for that occasion called "Assassination Raga." Other poets who read that night were Allen Ginsberg, Michael McClure, Lew Welch, Philip Whalen, and John Wieners. A decade later, Ferlinghetti wrote "An Elegy to Dispel Gloom" in response to yet two other political assassinations, those of Mayor Moscone and gay San Francisco supervisor Harvey Milk. He read that poem just across the street in a memorial held at the Civic Center.

In 1969, the Doors lead singer Jim Morrison and Michael McClure were in the Living Theatre's production of *Paradise Now* at the Nourse Auditorium. To portray Edenic innocence, the players removed all of their clothes. Perhaps the experience inspired Morrison in Miami later that year to replay his part. Charged with lewd and lascivious behavior in public, he was blacklisted from many auditoriums.

Walk back on Hayes to Van Ness and then turn left. Walk two blocks and stop in front of the Veterans Building on the southwest corner of McAllister Street.

San Francisco Museum of Modern Art 3.
401 Van Ness

Before the imposing new San Francisco Museum of Modern Art was built, modern art was exhibited in a much smaller museum on the fourth floor of the Veterans Auditorium. The San Francisco Art Association opened the museum in 1935, and it became a key venue of cultural events, including poetry readings. In 1952, when Dylan Thomas read at the art museum, all San Francisco's literati turned out to hear the great Welsh bard. Ferlinghetti's review in the *Chronicle* began "There is nothing like Dylan Thomas in poetry today."

In 1942, a fifteen-year-old high school student named Philip Lamantia came to the museum to see retrospectives of Salvador Dali and Joan Miró. Their work had such an impact that he began reading the Surrealists at the public library across the street and furiously writing poems at home. After some of them were published in the Surrealist magazines *View* and *VV* the following year, André Breton welcomed the young poet as "a voice that rises once in a hundred years."

Cross Van Ness and walk east on McAllister for one block to

CITY HALL. PHOTO BY BILL MORGAN

CAROLYN ROBINSON [CASSADY] AND NEAL CASSADY
AROUND THE TIME OF THEIR MARRIAGE IN SAN FRANCISCO.
PHOTO COURTESY OF CAROLYN CASSADY

City Hall and the Civic Center Plaza 4.
McAllister between Polk and Larkin

The elegant domed building is San Francisco's City Hall, which houses the Justice of the Peace. Here, Neal and Carolyn Cassady were married in a civil ceremony on April 1, 1948. Typical of what was to come, Carolyn had to come up with the $10 for the marriage license herself.

After *The Love Book* by poet Lenore Kandel was brought to trial on charges of obscenity in 1966, poet James Schevill organized a protest read-in of the book on the steps of City Hall. The book was indeed found obscene by the local court, but the ruling was overturned on appeal by the state supreme court. This was to be the city's last major obscenity trial for literature.

Directly across the plaza facing City Hall are two library buildings. The old library on the left has been renovated as an Asian arts museum. The new San Francisco Public Library is the building on the right.

San Francisco Public Library   5.
Civic Center at Larkin

In the spring of 1996 the San Francisco Public Library moved across the Grove Street Plaza from its beautiful old quarters to the postmodern building here. Many people believe that the new library provided space for everything except books and the architect's design has been the target of literary wrath from the beginning.

On the sixth floor of the library is the San Francisco history department with a small collection of material related to the Beat Generation. During the 1950s, the librarian responsible for local history didn't feel that Beat writings qualified as literature, and as a result the library missed an opportunity to gather materials. The universities in the area have done a much better job.

The old library lent a meeting room to Robert Duncan for a workshop he called "Poetry as Magic," which he led from 1957 to 1959. Every Tuesday night he allowed a maximum of fifteen people to come to his lectures. During those two years, Helen Adam, Robin Blaser, Ebbe Borregaard, Joe Dunn, Jack Gilbert, and George Stanley were among the regular attendees. The course was rooted in Duncan's deep interest in the application of magic to poetics through a variety of disturbances and passions. This was an approach not discussed in any textbook. In Helen Adam's play *Initiation to the Magic Workshop,* she offers a firsthand version of one of the workshop's sessions.

Continue east on McAllister past the libraries for one block to Hyde Street and turn left for another block and a half. Stop between Golden Gate and Turk in front of the

Motion Picture Studio and Laboratory 6.
125 Hyde

Jackie Gibson worked as an artist from 1959 to 1961 at the wonderful art deco Motion Picture Studio and Laboratory that stood here. During these years she had an off-again on-again relationship with Neal Cassady that finally ended when Cassady introduced her to Jack Kerouac, and she became involved with him for a brief period. Cassady wasn't very good at breaking off affairs and he was pleased when his lover went looking for a commitment elsewhere. Kerouac relates this entire affair in his depressingly honest book *Big Sur.*

Continue north on Hyde Street to the next corner with Turk. The vacant lot on the northeast corner was once the

Black Hawk nightclub 7.
200 Hyde

Evenings with Dave Brubeck, Cal Tjader, Gerry Mulligan Quartet, Errol Garner, Oscar Peterson, Shelley Manne, Charlie Mingus, and the Modern Jazz Quartet made the Black Hawk *the* jazz spot in the city during the 1950s. The place was a dump, but the people came for the jazz, the best in the world—from Billie Holiday to Miles Davis, who recorded his first live album here. Only an empty lot marks the site now. Johnny Noga and Guido Caccienti bought the club in 1949 and ran it until it closed in 1963. Poets and jazz aficionados Bob Kaufman, Jack Micheline, and Philip Lamantia came to listen to the music, and Kenneth Rexroth and Kenneth Patchen sometimes read poetry to jazz here. One night in 1959 Kaufman gave Billie Holiday a handful of poems written out in longhand, which she graciously accepted, probably without having any idea who he was.

Retrace your steps one block south on Hyde and then turn left on Golden Gate for one and a half blocks to the east. 150 Golden Gate was on the left side of the street facing the church.

Old Longshoremen's Hall (demolished in 2007) 8.
150 Golden Gate

The longshoremen's union had offices here until the new Longshoremen's Hall near Fisherman's Wharf was built in 1959. It was in this hall that Allen Ginsberg read his poem "Kaddish" to a crowd of about 200 people, the first public reading of what many critics consider to be his greatest poem. At the time it was one of the largest audiences to ever attend a poetry reading in the city; in the 1960s and 1970s, crowds reached the thousands.

Continue on Golden Gate to the next corner and turn left onto Jones Street for five blocks, stopping at Geary Street. Just on the left is the

PHOTO BY BILL MORGAN

Geary Hotel (now the Adante Hotel)   9.
610 Geary

On June 12, 1954, Allen Ginsberg visited San Francisco for the first time with his longtime friend and sometime lover, Neal Cassady. They stayed the night at the Geary Hotel and Ginsberg jotted notes in his journal so that he would remember the details of the place. "On the side-board—ring, watch, glasses, pack of trick cards, ashtray, *Bhaghavad Gita,* & postcard." After Cassady left, Ginsberg went out into the "cool, chilly almost, nite for first walk down theater bar Geary St. & chic looking S.F. first impressions." He lived in this hotel off and on during the fifties and sixties.

Walk back down Jones a block and turn left onto O' Farrell for a block and a half, stopping across from the Hilton Hotel in front of the giant parking garage where once stood the

Blackstone Hotel (now large parking lot)   10.
340 O'Farrell

Neal Cassady was sometimes an insensitive friend. In 1949, he drove cross-country from New York City with his first wife, Luanne, and his best friend, Jack Kerouac. When the three arrived in town after the long trip, Neal didn't know what to do with them because he was eager to see his current wife, Carolyn, alone and didn't need the complications of having his first wife along. So he simply coldly dropped them off here. Jack and Luanne had no money and no friends in San Francisco and had to fend for themselves. This sort of thing drove Luanne into the arms of more considerate and generous men, but neither she nor Kerouac ever stopped loving Neal.

Continue east on O' Farrell one half block to Mason and turn left for one and a half blocks just past Geary on the right side of the street to the

City Lights Poets Theatre   11.
420 Mason

When Kenneth Patchen died early in 1972, City Lights organized a memorial reading for him in this small theater in the very ornate Native Sons Building. On February 2, 1972, Robert Creeley, Lawrence Ferlinghetti, Robert Duncan, Charles Lipton, Morton Marcuse, Ishmael Reed, and Al Young mourned the poet-artist who had died in semi-obscurity in Palo Alto. The City Lights Poets Theatre, under the direction of Joe Krysiak, an impresario, graphic designer, and book packer at City Lights Publishers, presented plays and poetry readings here, among them an Ezra Pound memorial reading with Lenny Bruce, Robert Creeley, William Everson, Nanos Valaoritis, and many other luminaries.

Continue up the hill on Mason for another block and a half to Sutter. On the southwest corner you'll find

Marine's Memorial Theatre   12.
609 Sutter

Another "Tribute to Kenneth Patchen" was held nearly ten years earlier, on January 29, 1961, in the Marine's Memorial Theatre. Patchen had a crippling disease of the spine and this benefit was to help pay his medical bills. An all-star cast of readers performed on a brilliant stage set designed by Robert LaVigne. Among them were Helen Adam, James Broughton, Lawrence Ferlinghetti, Madeline Gleason, Michael McClure, Josephine Miles, Thomas Parkinson, and Philip Whalen. Kenneth Rexroth, as master of ceremonies, embarrassed himself by screaming in rage to Helen Adam that he didn't want to appear onstage with "a faggot tap dancer." (As it turned out the tap dancer had a wife and family in San Jose.) The auditorium in the Marine's Memorial Club and Hotel still has a variety of events throughout the year, faggot tap dancing included.

Walk up the hill one more block to Bush and turn left for a block to Taylor. On the north side of the street in the next block is the site of 952 Bush, now a large modern apartment complex.

The Say When Club 13.
952 Bush

Jack Kerouac wrote about jazz improviser Slim Gaillard in his book *On the Road*. Gaillard combined scat singing, zany humor, and inventive percussion in his act at places like The Say When Club, once located here in a row of now-vanished buildings. Kerouac wrote, "Slim Gaillard is a tall, thin Negro with big sad eyes who's always saying, 'Right-orooni' and 'How 'bout a little bourbon-oroooni.'" Gaillard reported that Kerouac was "a great listener . . . and that when I played The Say When Club, Jack showed up every night and stood with his back against the wall and while he listened, all the girls would cruise by and admire him. Between sets, I'd stand there right next to him. We were both so sharp we made a Gillette blade look like a hammer." The comedy stylings of Lord Buckley and Lenny Bruce owed a lot to the hip patter of Slim Gaillard and other black performers.

Turn up Taylor for one block north, then turn right on Pine for two and a half blocks; just past Powell in the middle of the block is a distinctive looking building.

Allen Ginsberg's apartment 14.
755 Pine

In 1954, Allen Ginsberg was twenty-eight and trying hard to be straight. He'd found a downtown job, he was dating girls, and he was going to a psychotherapist regularly. He moved into number 5 in this modest apartment building with his girlfriend, twenty-two year-old Sheila Williams, and her small child. Sheila wrote advertising copy for the May

SHEILA WILLIAMS AND SON.
PHOTO © ALLEN GINSBERG TRUST

134

755 PINE. PHOTO BY BILL MORGAN

Company and sang jazz by night. Allen wrote in his journal on October 12, 1954, "Depression now realizing after moving into this great Nob Hill apt. with Sheila that I 'don't love her' as 'she loves me' thus starving & killing her heart for my casual pleasure."

From his window in this apartment Ginsberg experienced the mighty presence of Moloch—the Old Testament god of the Ammonites and Phoenicians to whom children were sacrificed—which inspired his first masterpiece, "Howl."

You might want to cross the street and climb the stairs that are Joice Street. Looking back from the stairway you can see the older Medical Arts Building on the left but the modern hotel on the right blocks your view of the older Sir Francis Drake Hotel. It does give you an idea of how the lights of the buildings would have appeared to Ginsberg as he looked from his window on a gloomy, foggy night. When you pass the hotel itself in a few minutes, you'll be too close to it to see the upper-floor windows that so impressed Ginsberg. When you leave Joice Street, walk down the tiny block-long Dashiell Hammett Street just to the east of Ginsberg's Pine Street apartment. On the left side of the street halfway down at number 20 is an apartment building where Hammett lived. Although not one of the Beat writers, his detective novels influenced both Burroughs and Kerouac in their youth, and they both tried their hands at hard-boiled fiction. Cross to the other side of Bush and stop in the dead-end Burritt alleyway just across the street to the left from Dashiell Hammett Street. Look for a small

ALLEN GINSBERG AND PETER ORLOVSKY AT PINE AND POWELL, WITH THE SIR FRANCIS DRAKE HOTEL IN THE FOG.   PHOTO BY HARRY REDL

plaque on the wall of the building on the west side of the alley that marks the fictional site of the murder of Miles Archer, Sam Spade's partner, in The Maltese Falcon. *Then continue west on Bush back to Powell and turn left downhill one block to Sutter. You'll find the Sir Francis Drake Hotel at the corner of Sutter and Powell.*

Sir Francis Drake Hotel   15.
450 Powell

Anyone who has read Ginsberg's "Howl" is familiar with his powerful invocation of "the robot skullface of Moloch" and "Moloch whose eyes are a thousand blind windows!"

Few people realize that these images are based on his direct observation of the Gothic Sir Francis Drake Hotel. Ginsberg knew about Moloch, but it was only under the influence of peyote on the foggy night of October 17, 1954, that he actually beheld the terrible specter of an evil monster, a building from Hell, Moloch's building, in the upper stories of the Drake Hotel. Ginsberg described the inspiration in detail in *Howl: Original Draft Facsimile,* published thirty years later.

After writing the poem, Ginsberg went inside the Drake Hotel "to see the Starlite Room I been staring at from outside down below on street—Inside full of carpet & cocktail tables & bars. The French restaurant, Alouette—Sensation of belonging to the upper middle class on Sutter St. How pleasant & true to turn up the hill so near Drake-Sutter-Park-light—Trolley to Pine St. home alone." The Starlight Room is still on the twenty-first floor, but the Alouette restaurant is long gone.

Continue down Powell one block to Union Square. On the right you'll see the

St. Francis Hotel   16.
335 Powell

The Italian Renaissance Revival architecture and sumptuous interior of the expensive St. Francis Hotel makes it an unlikely stop on a tour of the Beat Generation. But it has a few Beat connections nonetheless. In 1952 Carolyn Cassady tried to get a job here when she lived on Russell Street in a ménage à trois with Jack and Neal. In 1966, the Colonial Room was the site of a "Teach-On LSD," a benefit for the Timothy Leary Defense Fund. Leary spoke on "The Politics and Ethics of Ecstasy." Big Brother and the Holding Company, the Sopwith Camel, Allen Ginsberg, David Meltzer, Michael McClure, and Richard Alpert also took part. Meltzer remembered meeting actor Peter Coyote that day for the first time. The event concluded with Peter Berg's cabaret play *Search and Seizure,* performed by the San Francisco Mime Troupe.

Continue down Powell Street one more block and stop in front of Kuletos in the lobby of the Villa Florence Hotel, the site of the old

Paddock (now Kuletos)   17.
221 Powell

One night to celebrate his new success, Jack Kerouac and a friend, Jay Blaise, stopped here. Kerouac bought drinks for two women who were sitting at the bar, but they ignored him. "I'm Jack Kerouac!" he informed them, only to be told, "Yeah? Well, fuck you!" A little later he tried again with two other women. He told them that he was Jay Blaise and, pointing to Blaise, said, "By the way, over there is Jack Kerouac." They immediately took off toward Blaise, and then told *him* to get lost, so they could be alone with "Kerouac." All this is related in Gerald Nicosia's biography of Kerouac, *Memory Babe*.

Continuing on Powell to the next corner, turn left on O' Farrell and stop in the next block at the corner of Stockton. On your left is

Macy's   18.
101 Stockton

A poem might come to a poet at any time and any place. Ferlinghetti wrote: "Looking in the mirrors at Macy's / and thinking it's a subterranean plot / to make me feel like Chaplin / snuck in with his bent shoes & beat bowler / looking for a fair-haired angel / Who's this bum / crept in off the streets / blinking in the neon / an anarchist among the floorwalkers / a strike-breaker even / right past the pickets / and the picket line is the People yet? / I think I'll hook a new derby / with my cane / and put a sign on it reading / Director of Alienation . . ."

Turn left up Stockton to the next corner, which is Geary, and stop at the southwest corner.

I. Magnin (now Louis Vuitton)   19.
Geary and Stockton

For several years, tourist buses brought people to North Beach to see exotic "beatniks" in their bohemian quarters, so one day, in retaliation, a group of North Beach bohemians marched to I. Magnin, an upscale Union Square department store, on "The Squaresville Tour." They pointed at clerks and customers, making commentaries on their peculiar dress and manners.

Continue up Stockton one block to Post. Turn right and then left onto Grant. Stop near the corner of Sutter. The White House was the large store on the southeast corner. Look for the name "The White House" between the second- and third-floor windows on the curved side of the building.

White House Department Store (now the Banana Republic) 20.
Grant between Sutter and Post

In 1948, Carolyn Cassady became pregnant before Neal was legally divorced from his first wife Luanne, so they weren't able to marry. When he finally got his divorce papers they wanted to tie the knot as quickly as possible. Neal asked a friend to buy the wedding ring for Carolyn and he arranged for her to meet his friend on this corner in front of the elegant White House store. Carolyn was led to believe that it would be a fine ring from the fashionable White House jewelry department. From where Carolyn stood she was able to see Neal's friend buy the ring at the Woolworth 5-and-10¢ store around the corner, then walk in the side door of the White House and come out through the front door so that it would appear that he had bought it there. It seemed fitting that they were married on April 1—April Fool's Day. Carolyn describes the scene in greater, and sadder, detail in her book *Off the Road*.

Ferlinghetti visited the White House cafeteria in his poem "Third World Calling." Unless you knew that the White House was a department store, you'd be convinced that the presidential residence in Washington has escalators and a perfume department. (Who knows, perhaps it does.)

POLK GULCH
TO THE FILLMORE

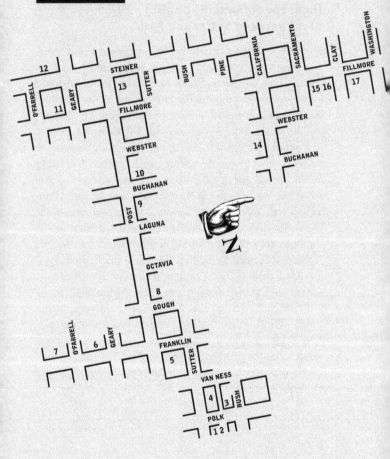

O'FARRELL
GEARY
STEINER
SUTTER
BUSH
PINE
CALIFORNIA
SACRAMENTO
CLAY
WASHINGTON
FILLMORE
12
11
13
FILLMORE
WEBSTER
15 16
17
WEBSTER
10
14
BUCHANAN
BUCHANAN
POST
9
LAGUNA
OCTAVIA
8
GOUGH
O'FARRELL
GEARY
FRANKLIN
7
6
5
SUTTER
VAN NESS
4 3
BUSH
POLK
1 2

POLK GULCH TO THE FILLMORE
and the Western Addition

Begin on the northeast corner of Polk and Sutter at the

Hotel Wentley   1.
1214 Polk

When the Montgomery Block building was torn down in 1959 to make way for the Transamerica Pyramid, many resident artists and writers moved to the Wentley, which became an incubator for artistic activity. The painter, Robert LaVigne, had been living at the Wentley as early as 1953 and the following year both Allen Ginsberg and Peter Orlovsky took up residence there for short periods.

One summer, printer Dave Haselwood lent his tiny room at the Wentley to poet John Wieners, who spent an entire week doing nothing but writing the poems that became *The Hotel Wentley Poems*. Haselwood published

HOTEL WENTLEY AND FOSTER'S CAFETERIA TODAY.   PHOTO BY BILL MORGAN

the poems as the very first book from his Auerhahn Press but he wasn't satisfied with the appearance of the book, which he had designed but not printed. Because of the idiocy of commercial printers (as he put it) he decided to become a fine-press printer himself.

On the first floor of the Wentley building was

Foster's Cafeteria   2.
1200 Polk

Ginsberg and his friends made this one of Foster's twenty-one cafeterias their own private hangout and it was here that Allen first met Robert LaVigne in 1954. The two began talking about the art scene in New York and hit it off at once. They were kindred spirits and remained fast friends for the rest of their lives. Through LaVigne, Ginsberg met Peter Orlovsky, as well as Michael and Joanna McClure. Although the Wentley building is still here, Foster's is long gone and the businesses are again under renovation.

Just to the north of the Wentley is Fern Street, and across Polk on the northwest corner was the

Hotel Young   3.
106 Fern

When his triangular relationship with Peter Orlovsky and Robert LaVigne became too emotionally tangled, Allen Ginsberg took a room by himself at the Hotel Young. He had fallen in love with Orlovsky and was in danger of scaring him away by his unrelenting passion and intense neediness. Ginsberg wanted to give him space but found it difficult. He asked for the corner room so he could watch for Orlovsky at Foster's Cafeteria across the street, then he could "accidentally" run into him. All during January 1955 Allen sat alone in his room and wrote long passages in his journal about his loneliness and love for Peter. A typical entry on January 2: "I sit up looking out window down on Polk & Sutter Foster's corner as if I might see him crossing street . . ." and later, "Woke up this morning in San Francisco in the rain a long way from home—a long way thru time—on hellish Sutter & Polk city corner —neons in the day, I was sick, outside my raindropped window, gray sky, huge USED CARS written on building-side (hovering like a ship in rain) ahead, . . ."

Neal Cassady stopped by a few times, and Ginsberg wrote in *Straight Hearts' Delight* "I can remember one of the last really wild times I made it with him, because I had a room of my own and there was privacy, finally. Finally things got too difficult for Orlovsky at LaVigne's and he moved into the Wentley." After a while Ginsberg and Orlovsky decided to share an apartment together on Montgomery Street in North Beach.

Turn west on Sutter Street and walk up the hill toward Van Ness where you will see on the north side of the street

Avalon Ballroom   4.
1268 Sutter

No particular Beat spirits are here, but you can note in passing the famous Avalon Ballroom, where between 1966 and 1968 thousands of San Franciscans rocked to the great shows produced by Chet Helms' Family Dog.

Continue west on Sutter, crossing Van Ness. You'll pass a marble building at 1335 Sutter on the south side of the street. A plaque on the facade commemorates Andrew Hoyem's Grabhorn Press, which issued several fine-press editions of Beat writers' work. Turn left on Franklin and stop near the parking garage where 1350 would have once stood.

Robert Duncan and Jess Collins's apartment 5.
1350 Franklin

The "Ghost House" was the nickname given to the spooky residence of poet Robert Duncan and artist Jess Collins in the 1950s. Now that the building has been demolished, it truly is a ghost. Duncan met Jess in Berkeley in 1950 and the two forged a solid relationship that lasted until Duncan's death in 1988. By the 1950s, the former Treadwell mansion at this location had begun to resemble the haunted houses in Charles Addams's cartoons. The once palatial house was divided into live-work spaces used by artists Martin Baer, Harry Jacobus, and Wally Hedrick, and the filmmaker, Stan Brakhage. Philip Lamantia lived here for a while with his first wife Goldian ("Gogo") Nesbit, a photographer. Duncan and Jess lived in what had once been the ballroom until the house was torn down in 1953.

Continue two blocks south on Franklin to Geary and stop on the southwest corner at the

First Unitarian Church 6.
1187 Franklin

Since 1889, when this neo-Gothic church was built, it has provided space for rousing lectures, readings, marriages (including one of Kenneth Rexroth's), and benefits for pacifist and humanitarian causes. In 1971, a symposium titled "Naturally High" brought Allen Ginsberg, the Kailas Shugendo Mantric Sun Band, Yogi Bhajan Ashram, and the Integral Yoga Institute together for a day of meditation and chanting. "Bring your own cushion," the poster suggested.

Continue one more block south on Franklin and stop in front of the Martin Luther Tower between O'Farrell and Ellis, near where 1041 Franklin once stood.

Natalie Jackson's apartment 7.
1041–1051 Franklin

On November 30, 1955, Neal Cassady's girlfriend, Natalie Jackson, jumped to her death from the roof of the apartment at 1051 Franklin. The building (and the whole

NATALIE JACKSON'S SUICIDE, NOVEMBER 30, 1955.
COURTESY OF *THE SAN FRANCISCO CHRONICLE*.

block) is gone, replaced by the Urban Life Center and Martin Luther Tower, but it was similar to the building still across the street at 1030 Franklin. Jackson had dated Cassady for about a year when Neal came up with a scheme for Natalie to impersonate his wife Carolyn. Under this guise they withdrew $10,000 from Carolyn's account, which Neal bet at the race track. He planned to double his money and replace the cash before Carolyn discovered it missing. The plan went smoothly, except the part about winning, and he lost the whole $10,000. Natalie was distraught over her part in the ruse. A few days later, Neal left her in Kerouac's care, but when Neal got home from work, he found that Natalie had slashed her throat and then run from the roof of her apartment at 1041 Franklin across several attached roofs to 1051 Franklin, where she fell to her death while trying to elude a police officer who was trying to help her. Cassady and Kerouac were terrified of being implicated and denied that they knew who she was. In the *Dharma Bums,* Kerouac recounted the tragedy as he saw it.

Retrace your steps north on Franklin to Post and turn left one block to Gough. Turn right and stop in front of 1401–05 Gough.

"NUDE WITH ONIONS," ROBERT LAVIGNE'S PORTRAIT OF PETER ORLOVSKY THAT GINSBERG FELL IN LOVE WITH IN 1954. COURTESY OF ROBERT LAVIGNE

Robert LaVigne's apartment 8.
1403 Gough

One day in 1954, painter Robert LaVigne brought Ginsberg here to see his paintings. One of them, *Nude with Onions,* which hung opposite the front entry of his studio, depicted a nude boy sitting on a divan. Ginsberg was entranced. A few minutes later the real-life model, Peter Orlovsky, entered the studio and Ginsberg met the man who would become his life's companion. Ginsberg remembered the moment clearly until the day he died. He wrote, "There was this giant picture there, over the fireplace, a very beautiful portrait of Peter, naked, with a Greek kind of drapery around him. And something happened sort of between me and it; that is, like I fell in love with it, and so I was delighted a few minutes later when

ROBERT LAVIGNE.   PHOTO BY LARRY KEENAN

Peter actually walked in the room." Shortly afterward Ginsberg wrote one of his most important autobiographical poems, "Malest Cornifici Tuo Catullo" in which he addressed Kerouac. "I'm happy, Kerouac, your madman Allen's finally made it: discovered a new young cat, and my imagination of an eternal boy walks on the streets of San Francisco, handsome, and meets me in cafeterias and loves me . . ." In December, Ginsberg moved in with LaVigne and Orlovsky. It didn't work out well, and after some jealous arguments that Ginsberg called "great magical personality hassles," he moved to the Hotel Young on New Year's Day 1955.

This apartment was passed along from friend to friend, and Ginsberg returned to stay here almost ten years later in 1963. He wrote to Orlovsky, "I'm living at 1403 Gough St. (!!!) with bunch of young Kansas poets, David

Haselwood of Auerhahn Press is upstairs, Neal Cassady and his girl Anne [Murphy] is in one room also. He's started writing . . . Robert Frank was here & we worked out film treatment for *Kaddish*." He also noted that Michael McClure was there and a young poet from Kansas named Charles Plymell. "Gee what a weird huge apartment this is," he wrote.

Return to the corner of Post and turn west walking over the hill for three blocks, stopping near Buchanan in the center of Japantown for the next two sites. Nothing remains of the buildings, but what went on here is important to the story of the Beats.

Jackson's Nook / Jimbo's Bop City   9.
1638 Buchanan / 1690 Post

The Fillmore district was where the Beats came to hear the exciting new jazz known as bebop. Two clubs in particular outshone the rest and Kerouac mentions them by name in his novels. Jackson's Nook at 1638 Buchanan was an early favorite of Kerouac, Cassady, and Al Hinkle during the days of their *On the Road* adventures. Lamantia recalled that not only was the music terrific but that Jackson's Nook served the best soul food in town. Another great venue was Bop City, an after-hours club once at 1690 Post. At 2 A.M., working musicians would begin to drop in after their paying gigs were over for the night. Here they could just sit back and jam whenever they felt like it, and it was also one of the few places in town where black and white musicians could play together. From the day it opened in 1950, the jazz here was always cutting edge. Jimbo's didn't have a liquor license, and the owner, Jimbo Edwards, ran the place as a waffle shop by day. Jazz greats like Frank Foster, Dexter Gordon, and Billie Holiday all came around. Louis Armstrong stopped by in 1952 to listen to Charlie Parker, maybe the only time these two giants ever met. In "Time Traveler's Potlatch" Lamantia envisioned "the cinematic projection from a hummingbird's eye of Charlie Parker's spontaneous musical session at Bop City, San Francisco in 1954, fixed in an order of black, white and red crystallizations volatilizing the human brain on the brink of an evolutionary mutation."

Both Jackson's Nook and Bop City were torn down to make way for Japantown in 1968.

Also demolished for Japantown was a row of buildings connected by balconies that stood here on the west side of Buchanan, on the north side of Post.

Hyphen House / Gavin Arthur / Borregaard's Museum 10.
1713–1703 Buchanan

The Hyphen House was a communal apartment organized to introduce people to Asian cultures. When the East-West House on California Street ran out of space, this house was rented as a kind of annex, and named the Hyphen House (for the hyphen between East and West).

George Stanley and Ebbe Borregaard moved here in 1960 and, after the Hyphen House closed, installed Borregaard's Museum and Art Gallery. The idea was to use a gallery for poetry readings, lectures, and run an alternative school along the lines of Black Mountain College. The enterprise never really succeeded, but some ace readings were held in the gallery.

Gavin Arthur, a grandson of President Chester A. Arthur, lived at 1703 Buchanan from 1966 until the buildings were torn down. He was a "Spiritual Counselor," according to his business card, an astrologist, and a companion of the Beats. He taught a course in comparative religion and philosophy at San Quentin Prison while Neal Cassady was serving time there and became a close friend. When Cassady was released, he lived with Arthur briefly. Allen Ginsberg loved to tell people about his sexual connection with Walt Whitman. He insisted that Whitman had a sexual relationship with Edward Carpenter, who had one with Gavin Arthur, who had one with Neal Cassady, who then had one with Ginsberg. Although some scholars are uncertain about whether Whitman ever acted on his homosexual passions, Ginsberg was convinced that he had, and this tenuous connection was very important to him.

Continue west on Post to Fillmore and turn left one block to Geary. Across the bridge on the southwest corner is

Fillmore Auditorium   11.
1805–1807 Geary

This building was once used as a union hall by the Association of Amalgamated Labor and then as a concert hall and dance school called the Majestic Hall and Academy of Dancing. In the late 1940s Jack Kerouac came to a club here to listen to jazz and wrote about it in *On the Road*. But the hall will always be remembered as the Fillmore Auditorium, where Bill Graham presented nearly 300 rock concerts and light shows between 1966 and 1968. Graham found the second-floor auditorium while looking for a place to stage a second San Francisco Mime Troupe benefit in 1965. Not just musical history was made at the Fillmore; shortly before his death Lenny Bruce gave his last performance here on June 26, 1966.

There were plenty of literary events, too. In 1966 Andrei Voznesensky read his poetry in Russian, with Ferlinghetti reading English translations. Michael McClure's play *The Beard* found a very temporary home here when it was suppressed for obscenity by the police at another theater. Although the play won two Obies in New York City, San Francisco authorities threatened to revoke Graham's permit if he allowed more than a single performance, so after only one performance *The Beard* had to move to The Committee in North Beach. LeRoi Jones's play *The Dutchman* was also staged at the Fillmore, with the same kind of harassment.

Stay on Fillmore for one more block south, then turn right onto O' Farrell for one block, and go to the park across Steiner Street.

Labaudt Gallery   12.
1497 Steiner

In 1947 Madeline Gleason began the Festival of Contemporary Poetry at the small Labaudt Gallery that once stood where you see the athletic field on the west side of the street. With the help of Robert Duncan and James Broughton, Gleason created a local poetry festival, of which Broughton said, "it was poetry, music and painting—a whole burst of creative energy" that galvanized the writing community. When the audiences grew too large for the gallery, she moved the festival to the San Francisco Museum of Art.

Walk back to Geary on Steiner, carefully crossing this busy intersection, and stop on the northeast corner of Post and Steiner.

Winterland 13.
1725 Steiner

Winterland, the legendary ice rink turned auditorium, was torn down in 1985 and is now the site of a condominium development. The millions of fans of the Band remember this as the site of the rock group's first public performance in 1969, after they recorded the *Music from Big Pink* album. The Band's final performance was also given here on Thanksgiving Day 1976, and was filmed by Martin Scorcese and released as *The Last Waltz,* one of the best concert films ever. Musicians Eric Clapton, Neil Diamond, Dr. John, Ronnie Hawkins, Joni Mitchell, Van Morrison, Ringo Starr, Muddy Waters, and Neil Young were joined on stage by poets Lawrence Ferlinghetti and Michael McClure.

Producer Bill Graham used Winterland for larger concerts and recording sessions after he closed Fillmore West in 1971. It could hold 5,400 people, and throughout the 1970s Graham filled every seat. There was one quasi-literary event scheduled that never did take place: Ken Kesey's Acid Graduation on Halloween 1966. Graham canceled the show, bowing to political pressure; he took chances with music but not with his promoter's license.

Continue four blocks up Steiner and turn east onto California for two and a half blocks, stopping just past Webster at

East-West House 14.
2273 California

The East-West House was designed to introduce Asian customs and traditions to Westerners. Students from Alan Watts's failed American Academy of Asian Studies opened the doors in the mid-1950s, and during its early years, writers Lenore Kandel, Joanne Kyger, Albert Saijo, Lew Welch, and Philip Whalen all lived here. Joanne Kyger took up residence in May 1959 to prepare for her trip to

Japan the following February. She planned merely to visit Gary Snyder, but ended up marrying him in Japan. At the East-West House Kyger began a lifelong practice of meditation. She felt an affinity with other people in the house and got to know Lew Welch and Claude Dalenberg. Residents divided up cooking and cleaning chores.

PHOTO BY BILL MORGAN

EAST-WEST HOUSE.

Not everyone went on to Japan. In 1959 Jack Kerouac stayed here a while, and then headed back east with Welch and Saijo to be home for Thanksgiving. When the three arrived in New York they collaborated on the long poem published as *Trip Trap*. Kerouac's biographer, Gerald Nicosia said that the East-West House "was no placid colony of self-contained workers" but rather "a madhouse of Zen lunatics."

Walk back to Fillmore on California and turn right up the hill, stopping in the middle of the block between Clay and Sacramento.

Batman Gallery   15.
2222 Fillmore

William Jahrmarkt, a wealthy young friend of Michael McClure, was a fanatical enthusiast of Batman comic books. When he decided to start a gallery, McClure suggested that he call it after his hero, Batman, and Jahrmarkt did. Jahrmarkt had something else to thank McClure for too. Jahrmarkt's father, who controlled the family purse strings, didn't want to advance money to his bohemian son until McClure convinced him that a gallery would keep him out of trouble. The gallery opened on November 3, 1960, with walls painted black by Bruce Conner, and a poetry reading by Kirby Doyle. "Billy Batman," as Jahrmarkt came to be known, presented McClure's play *!The Feast!* here the following month, with actors Robert LaVigne, Ron Loewinsohn, Joanna McClure, David

JOANNE KYGER IN INDIA. PHOTO © ALLEN GINSBERG TRUST

Meltzer, Morton Subotnick, and Philip Whalen, all wearing tissue paper beards and speaking in McClure's "beast language." According to McClure, the people who hung out at the gallery "were more like gypsies than anything. They were civilized and screwy. They picked up their lifestyle from Robert Duncan and Wallace Berman, and they were dedicated to art." The gallery was sold in 1962 to Michael Agron, who ran it until 1965. Over the years they showed work by avant-garde artists, including Robert Branaman, Joan Brown, Bruce Conner, Jay DeFeo, Wally Hedrick, George Herms, and Charles Plymell. As you see, this neighborhood hangout has been eaten by Starbuck's.

Next door was once the

International Music Hall   16.
2226A Fillmore

The International Music Hall at 2226A Fillmore had a ballroom on the second floor with hardwood floors and a small stage that was occasionally used for poetry readings. Neighbor Michael McClure read his "Ghost Tantras" here for the first time. A benefit for the Auerhahn Press was held on November 26, 1963. For $1 you could hear Ginsberg, McClure, Meltzer, Welch, Whalen, and printer/poet Andrew Hoyem read from their latest work. The publishers of Auerhahn books, Dave Haselwood and Andrew Hoyem, were printing at 1605 Laguna (a building that has since been torn down) on a Hartford letterpress, an old fin-de-siecle machine. Haselwood learned the fine art of printing while holding down a steady job at the post office. He started the press to publish some of the powerful manuscripts he had been seeing around San Francisco that were going unnoticed. "I wanted to see them in print, not in five years but immediately," he said. The 1963 benefit helped keep the press afloat for another two years, at which time Haselwood turned it over to Andrew Hoyem, the founder of its successor, the Grabhorn Press.

Continue walking north on Fillmore one more block and stop in front of

Michael and Joanna McClure's flat   17.
2324 Fillmore

From 1958 to 1961 Michael and Joanna McClure lived in a very large flat here. McClure described the neighborhood in those days as a no-man's-land. It wasn't especially dangerous, he said, but it just wasn't part of any neighborhood—not the wealthy white Pacific Heights district up the hill or the poor black Fillmore district down the hill. "[It was] a boundary between two bio-areas, and it had the complexity and richness of an ecotone. Thrift shops enriched by the wealthy and a lovely park for the gentry, where I could take the peyote given to me by Wallace Berman, and only a short walk to black butcher shops and jazz clubs and grocery stores and music instrument shops."

Kenneth Rexroth and Jess Collins helped them move in, and even lugged a massive stove up the stairs. They had to install electrical fixtures themselves because previous tenants took everything when they left, even the light switches. The McClures had so many rooms that some had no more in them than a single plant on the bare wooden floors, but the walls were soon covered with art. Joanna McClure wrote her first poem in this apartment in 1958. Called "Dear Lover," it's one of her most romantic poems.

The McClures bridged the gap between the art and the literary worlds; their home was always open to visitors, and they hosted huge parties. John Wieners spent much time here, sometimes baby-sitting with McClure's daughter, Jane, and it was there that Robert LaVigne drew the portraits of Wieners used in the first edition of *The Hotel Wentley Poems*. "Poem for the Dead I Know" was written on McClure's roof around the same time.

Diane di Prima stayed with the McClures in 1961 on her first visit to San Francisco. During her first week in the city, she met with many authors whose work she had been publishing in her *Floating Bear* newsletter. Philip Lamantia and Philip Whalen were frequent guests at the McClures, and both wrote poems about their daughter, who is referred to in the poems as "The Boobus." Neal Cassady came by once, trying to sell them a new Nash automobile for $75. Even Aldous Huxley once dropped in. Poet Kirby Doyle came around when he was writing "Happiness Bastard," which Michael considers one of the best satires ever written.

Artist Jay DeFeo lived and worked downstairs in the same building with her husband, painter Wally Hedrick, at 2322 Fillmore. She painted her monumental masterpiece, *The Rose,* over a period of many years in her studio here. The painting weighed thousands of pounds and had to be removed with a crane when the time came to take it out. DeFeo died tragically, poisoned by the huge quantities of white lead paint she used. Artist Joan Brown lived in still another apartment in this building and often entertained Elmer Bischoff, Willem De Kooning, David Parks, and other contemporary artists.

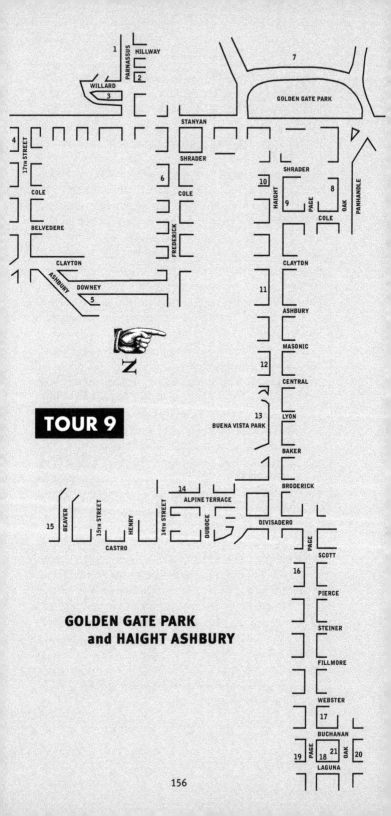

TOUR 9

GOLDEN GATE PARK
and HAIGHT ASHBURY

PHILIP WHALEN HOLDING HIS PORTRAIT BY MICHAEL MCCLURE.
PHOTO BY LARRY KEENAN

GOLDEN GATE PARK
AND HAIGHT-ASHBURY

Take the number 6 Parnassus bus to the starting point of this tour. First stop is at the UCSF Medical Center, opposite the end of Hillway Street.

Philip Hicks's office   1.
401 Parnassus

In 1954, when Allen Ginsberg was aspiring to be a middle-class businessman, he was in therapy with a young psychiatrist by the name of Philip Hicks. Dr. Hicks's office was at the Langley Porter Clinic, an extension of UC Berkeley's

Medical School. At one point the doctor asked him, "What would you really like to do?" Ginsberg said that he would like to do nothing but write poetry, spend all day with friends, and visit museums. Hicks replied, "Well, why don't you?" It was almost as easy as that. Within a few months Ginsberg quit his marketing research job, chose the life of a gay poet, and never looked back.

Walk down Parnassus east toward the city to

Hunter S. Thompson's apartment 2.
318 Parnassus

One of the wildest descendants of the Beat Generation, Hunter S. Thompson housed his hip consciousness in

the stucco building with the oval window during the mid-sixties. Thompson was writing his first book, *Hell's Angels,* when he met Allen Ginsberg and William Burroughs. Ginsberg and Ken Kesey had acquaintances among the Hell's Angels, and Michael McClure was helping Frank Reynolds write his own insider's look at the Angels, *Freewheelin' Frank.* Thompson dug motorcycles and spent much time riding his bike along the coast highway late into the nights. He rode high, low, and easy.

Turn right up steep Willard Street for a block and a half. On the east side is a gray wooden house.

Ruth Witt-Diamant's house 3.
1520 Willard

While living here in 1954, Ruth Witt-Diamant created the San Francisco Poetry Center at San Francisco State College, one of the country's great poetry institutions. Many poets, legendary or unknown, came to her frequent parties at this house, among them Dylan Thomas, W. H. Auden, Elizabeth Bishop, Robert Lowell, Anaïs Nin, Theodore Roethke, and Stephen Spender.

Jack Kerouac wrote a long passage about a crazy dinner party at Witt-Diamant's in *Desolation Angels*. He disguises her as Rose Wise Lazuli, and writes that she has "those serious woman eyes that get all liquid and bedroom eyes even in middle age, it denotes a lover-soul."

Louise Bogan, Malcolm Cowley, Randall Jarrell, and William Carlos Williams helped initiate the Poetry Center with early readings there. Jarrell heard the young Gregory Corso read there in 1956 and was so impressed that he invited him to stay at his home in Washington, D.C. Corso was delighted to accept, but before too long the patrician Jarrell had to invent an excuse to move the irrepressible Corso out.

Retrace your steps down Willard to Parnassus and turn right for two blocks. At Stanyan turn right again and walk south for four blocks to 17th Street. Turn left on 17th and stop midway between Stanyan and Schrader.

Helen Adam's place   4.
4927 17th Street

Poet Helen Adam, a native of Glasgow, Scotland, moved to San Francisco in 1953. She associated with filmmaker Stan Brakhage and later Robert Duncan at his Magic Workshops at the public library, where she shared her vatic knowledge of Scottish and British ballads. Her play *Initiation to the Magic Workshop* captures the spirit of those workshops and the characters who attended. In 1957 Adams formed her own group, the Maidens, devoted to magic and poetry. They were a gay bunch, including Robin Blaser, James Broughton, Jess Collins, Robert Duncan, Madeleine Gleason, and Eve Triem. Adam's performances were wonderful events in which she sang and chanted her poems in her rough Scottish brogue. People considered her a kind of godmother to this San Francisco Renaissance.

Follow 17th Street up the hill for three blocks and turn left on Clayton. One block ahead bear right onto Ashbury and then turn left to

MICHAEL MCCLURE AND JOANNA MCCLURE. PHOTO BY LARRY KEENAN

Michael and Joanna McClure's house 5. 264 Downey

Joanna and Michael McClure moved to this shingle-sided house in 1967 and for more than two decades they entertained just as much here as they had at their apartment on Fillmore Street. McClure described it as "a farm house in the sky, with two fireplaces, avocado and redwood trees in the back, and out the front, the world's greatest view of the ocean, the sky and Mount Tamalpais. I sat there at my desk looking at that as I wrote *The Beard*." That play went through acrimonious battles with the censors. At nearly every performance the play would be shut down and forced to move on to a different theater.

"In back," McClure said about this house, "we had raccoons and salamanders in the leaf mulch, it was only a six block walk to the top of Twin Peaks where there were sparrow hawks and a flock of band-tailed pigeons. It was a three block walk downhill to the Psychedelic Shop, and in the early innocent days my preteen daughter would walk down there and buy a bead or button and walk home." At this house McClure pursued his theater work, wrote several books of poetry, and developed his "beast language" and "poetry as biology" theories. Joanna McClure began writing poetry here, which was published in her first book, *Wolf Eyes,* in 1974.

Continue one long block down Downey Street to Frederick and turn left for two and a half blocks passing Cole Street. Look for a gray Victorian house on the south side of the street.

Kay Boyle's apartment 6.
419 Frederick

Poet and novelist Kay Boyle was born in St. Paul, Minnesota, in 1902. She grew up in Cincinnati and New York, then spent nearly twenty years in France. She moved to San Francisco in 1963 and taught at San Francisco State College until her retirement in 1979. This Victorian was for many years her home. In 1967 Boyle and Ferlinghetti were busted at the Oakland Army Induction Center while protesting the Vietnam War. She dared Ferlinghetti to get arrested—and he did, along with Boyle, Joan Baez's mother, and many students. Some refused to be bailed out and Ferlinghetti spent nineteen days in jail. Robert Treuhaft, the husband of Jessica Mitford, was the lawyer who defended him and many others, preventing worse sentences. Boyle's novel about the student protest movement, *The Underground Woman,* was published in 1975.

Continue on Frederick to the next large street, Stanyan, and turn right along the sidewalk bordering Golden Gate Park. Enter the park to the west at one of the walkways.

Golden Gate Park 7.
"Hippie Hill" near Kezar Drive

On the top of a sloping green hill, just off Kezar Drive, there's a pleasant panoramic view. This was the backyard of the Haight-Ashbury in the 1960s, where news from the counterculture was spread by flyers and word of mouth. On any given day the Communications Company might have been seen handing out free poems, playing music, dancing, smoking pot, picnicking, and throwing Frisbees.

The park had earlier inspired Lawrence Ferlinghetti to write a poem that begins, "In Golden Gate Park that day / a man and his wife were coming along / thru the enormous meadow / which was the meadow of the world / He was wearing green suspenders / and carrying an old beat-up flute / in one hand. . . ."

Exit the park along the road in front of the administration building that comes out on Oak Street, the south side of the Panhandle. Walk along Oak for two blocks to

Diane di Prima's flat 8.
1915 Oak

As soon as Diane di Prima laid her New York eyes on San Francisco in 1961, she wanted to live here. She remembered that, "in those days it was like you had fallen into a fairy tale. Even in the ghetto the buildings were beautiful." Her main reasons for the move were "to study with Suzuki Roshi and to work with the Diggers." In 1967, when she first visited the city, she stayed with Lenore

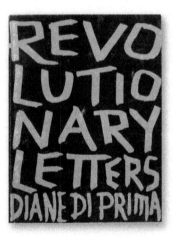

Kandel on Chestnut Street in North Beach. In June of the following year, she moved to Oak Street, where she paid the $300 rent and shared the flat with several others. On the Panhandle across the street, the Diggers were providing the basic needs of life for free: food, clothing, and shelter. Many Digger activists like Peter Coyote, Emmet Grogan, Peter Berg, and Lenore Kandel hung out at Diane's house. Di Prima's *Revolutionary Letters* were written here and syndicated through the Liberation News Service. They were widely read in the underground press before being gathered together as a City Lights book.

DIANE DIPRIMA.

Philip Whalen and di Prima became close friends and he shared his knowledge of the natural history of California with her. At one point the landlord wanted to sell her the whole house for $35,000 but she couldn't get the $10,000 down payment together. Later, di Prima moved to the country in response to the continual surveillance by the FBI, who had targeted her house for investigation of purported revolutionary activities (get-togethers of the Black Panthers and the White Panthers, for instance).

Turn right on Cole and walk two blocks south to Haight. On the northwest corner of Cole and Haight is the

Straight Theater (now a Goodwill store) 9.
1702 Haight

Haight Street was the center of the hippie movement that came to flower after the Beats had dispersed for other parts in the 1960s. The Beat writers continued to have a major influence on the culture but they were nearly twenty years older than the kids now flocking to San Francisco. The Straight Theater at 1702 Haight Street bridged the generation gap through its productions and events. Once Kenneth Rexroth read poetry here along with fifteen-year-old Jessica Hagedorn, now a celebrated performance artist and author of many books. The Living Theatre staged a free performance of *Paradise Now* at the Straight, involving the audience in the action as they always did, but the people outside on the street were living their own *Paradise Now,* and upstaged the theater group.

Walk west on Haight and on the other side of the street just before Shrader is an old three-story building.

The Diggers   10.
1775 Haight

A group of radical optimists promoting the idea that everyone deserved free food and clothing called themselves the Diggers after English agrarian Communists of the mid-seventeenth century. Both the old and new Diggers tried to set up an alternative economic system not dependent on money. They had many headquarters over the years; this particular one was ambitiously described in an issue of the *San Francisco Oracle:* "The Diggers have opened a new storefront to establish and operate a restaurant, sell farm produce, shelter people in need of rooms, repair cars and make tents for use in the parks and countryside." Along with the *Oracle,* the Diggers were sponsors of the 1967 Human Be-In in Golden Gate Park, which presaged the so-called Summer of Love. Their building on Haight Street is still here, but the Diggers are long gone. One of the leaders of the Diggers, Emmett Grogan, wrote about the movement in his underground classic, *Ringolevio.*

Retrace your steps east on Haight for three blocks to the

Psychedelic Shop
(now a pizza restaurant)   11.
1535 Haight

On January 3, 1966, the Psychedelic Shop opened here and became the "neighborhood general store" for the hippie phenomenon. It was founded by two brothers, Ron and Jay Thelin, whose father managed a Woolworth's across the street. The brothers planned to sell books, records, and magazines to the youth who were streaming into the neighborhood. Thus was founded the first head shop in the area, offering psychedelic posters, concert tickets, and drug paraphernalia. There was a large community bulletin board inside, and a meditation room (although, someone said, much of the meditation was centered "on your partner's naked body"). They took theater seats from the Straight Theater and set them in the front window facing the street so the regulars could sit and watch the passing scene.

On November 17, 1966, a police vice squad raided the Psychedelic Shop, looking for Lenore Kandel's allegedly obscene poem, *The Love Book,* and they found several copies for sale. The editor of the *Oracle,* Allen Cohen, was working as the store clerk that day and he was arrested. After a five-week trial, *The Love Book* was found obscene, but the decision was eventually reversed on appeal. The first printing of Kandel's book, which had sold less than fifty copies prior to the bust, quickly sold out and had to be reprinted numerous times. She donated some of her royalties to the police retirement fund as an ironic thank-you for their unwitting help.

Continue along Haight for two more blocks and stop just past Masonic at

The *Oracle* office 12.
1371 Haight

The late 1960s saw the birth of an underground press movement unrivaled in American history. The *San Francisco Oracle* was one of the first of these early counterculture newspapers that included the *Berkeley Barb,* the *Los Angeles Free Press, and* the *East Village Other.* The *Oracle* office moved several times, but from the sixth number until its demise, editors Allen Cohen and Michael Bowen published in this building. The paper was printed in psychedelic colors in tabloid format, featuring utopian stories and poetry by such writers as Dick Alpert, Lawrence Ferlinghetti, Philip Lamantia, Allen Ginsberg, Jerry Rubin, Gary Snyder, and Lew Welch. One of the *Oracle*'s great pieces was a long interview with Allen Ginsberg, Timothy Leary, Gary Snyder, and Alan Watts, published under the title "Changes" in the February 1967 issue. It tried to define the social and political ideals of an entire generation and it did just that. Although the *Oracle* lasted only from 1966 until 1968, it was such an important and beautifully produced paper that a facsimile edition was published for its twenty-fifth anniversary in 1992. This edition sold out at several hundred dollars a copy and is now a collectors' item.

Continue walking east on Haight Street one more block to

Buena Vista Park   13.
Haight and Baker

Just as North Beach had became a tourist mecca, attracting wannabees and gawkers, so did Haight-Ashbury. Tour buses looking for hippies began to outnumber local cars on Haight Street. To mark the end of an era and to protest the commercialization of their neighborhood, the locals staged a "Death of Hippie" funeral on October 6, 1967, in Buena Vista Park. Sunrise services were held for "Hippie, devoted son of Mass Media," and he was carried to his grave in a casket filled with beads, flowers, and hash brownies. The group symbolically buried the Psychedelic Shop's sign here in Buena Vista Park. They picked this date, October 6, because that was the day a year earlier that the State of California outlawed the use of LSD. From that moment on, things went underground. People who had legally taken LSD on October 5 became criminals on October 6.

Continue down Haight two blocks to Broderick, and turn right on Broderick then left on Waller and right on Alpine. Continue up the steep hill to

Neal and Carolyn Cassady's house   14.
160 Alpine Terrace

Carolyn Cassady found a house at the top of the steep stairway here and moved into it in June 1948. She lived to regret the choice of this place, as she described it in *Off the Road*. She was pregnant with Cathleen Joanne Cassady at the time, and the walk up the hill was a challenge. For the most part, Neal wasn't much help with domestic matters. He wrote to Allen Ginsberg in May 1948, shortly after Carolyn told him she was pregnant. "My mind doesn't function properly. The child and Carolyn are removed from my consciousness and are on a somehow, secondary plane, or i.e. not what I think of, or dwell on, or am concerned about, except in a secondary way."

Continue south on Alpine Terrace to 14th Street and turn left to Castro Street. Turn right on Castro to Beaver Street and stop at

PHILIP WHALEN AND ALLEN GINSBERG, 1971.   PHOTO BY GORDON BALL
©GORDON BALL

Philip Whalen's apartment   15.
123 Beaver

Whalen lived in a downstairs apartment here in 1963, where Richard Brautigan, Allen Ginsberg, and Lew Welch visited him. The kitchen and bathroom were shared with the other apartments and one biographer joked that Whalen moved into the front room of the house and gradually worked his way back, room by room, until he lived next to the kitchen. "Food, it would seem, is his sustenance, his security, his pastime, his faith in the future," said a friend. Another friend that lived and wrote here was David Kherdian, who compiled the first bibliography of Whalen's writings and wrote about many of San Francisco's poets. It's hard to imagine anyone not liking the genial Whalen, but Jack Spicer was such a person. Once when someone told Spicer that they had paid Whalen $10 to read at the San Francisco State College Poetry Festival, Spicer said that he'd pay him $11 *not* to read.

Return to Castro Street and walk back up 14th and Duboce Streets. Bear left where Castro turns into Divisidero and, once over the hill, turn off Divisidero onto Page Street. Stop at

Kenneth Rexroth's apartment 16. 250 Scott

The Victorian building on the corner of Page looks ancient enough to have some history behind it, and it does. Here Kenneth Rexroth lived from 1956 until 1968 in a large seven-room apartment on the second floor over Jack's Record Shop. He had an influential book program on KPFA/FM, and hosted a weekly Friday night salon here. These Friday nights were a gathering of the city's poetic intelligentsia, and Rexroth sounded off authoritatively on every imaginable subject from anarchism to Zen, always dominating the discussions with strong opinions. He espoused a kind of philosophical anarchism, heavily spiced with Wobbly populist ideas. Among the many writers who dropped in to take part were James Broughton, Robert Duncan, William Everson, Lawrence Ferlinghetti, Jack Kerouac, Philip Lamantia, Michael McClure, David Meltzer, Richard Moore, Thomas Parkinson, and Muriel Rukeyser. Ginsberg heard Rexroth read his great poem, "Thou Shalt Not Kill" at one of the weekly soirees. Rexroth once told David Meltzer that Kerouac was shocked when he "walked into my house, sat down in a kind of stiff-legged imitation of a lotus posture, and announced he was a Zen Buddhist . . . and then discovered everyone in the room knew at least one Oriental language." That was overstating the case; some pointed out that Rexroth himself didn't really know "oriental languages" either—and he was translating from them.

Continue east on Page for four blocks. On the north side of the street between Webster and Buchanan you'll find

Diane di Prima's flat 17.
452 Page

In 1970, after Diane di Prima's divorce from Alan Marlowe, she moved to the top floor of this house. At the time the neighborhood thundered with black revolutionary spirit, and di Prima dug this and the people she met here. Her new husband, Graham Fischer, fixed up this abandoned building in exchange for a modest rent. While he worked on it, di Prima became pregnant with her son, Rudi. Diane had been interested in Zen Buddhism, having devoured Paul Rep's collection of Zen and pre-Zen writings called *Zen Flesh, Zen Bones*. Most mornings from five to six, she would go for sitting meditation in an old church several blocks away on California Street. Although most of the members of the church were Buddhists from Asia, she was surprised that only the non-Asians seemed to practice sitting meditation.

Continue down Page a block and a half to the

Zen Center of San Francisco 18.
300 Page

Beat Generation writers like Kerouac, Ginsberg, Snyder, Whalen, Welch, Kyger, and di Prima all practiced various forms of Buddhism. Members of the Japanese community invited Suzuki Roshi to open a Buddhist center here for the performance of traditional weddings and other ceremonies needed by Japanese residents. The center quickly attracted young Westerners interested in learning how to meditate. In 1973 poet Philip Whalen became a longtime member of the sangha here. In exchange for room and board, Baker Roshi asked him to teach at the center. Thus Whalen was ordained Unsui (Zen Buddhist monk) and in 1975 became Shuso (head monk) at the Zen Mountain Center at Tassajara Springs. Other friends of the Zen Center have included Robert Duncan, Gregory Bateson, Stewart Brand, and Sym Van der Ryn, who became the director of the Farralones Institute. Inside this fine old brick building, you'll find a good Buddhist bookstore on the first floor. A seminal book by Rick Fields, *How the Swans Came to the Lake,* traces the birth of Buddhism in America and its influence on American literature. Other

ALLEN GINSBERG, MICHAEL MCCLURE, AND BRUCE CONNER, 1965
PHOTO BY LARRY KEENAN

businesses established by the Zen Center over the years
have included the Tassajara Bakery, the Alaya Stitchery,
Greens Vegetarian Restaurant (still in operation at Fort
Mason), and the Whole Earth Bookstore.

Turn right at the corner of Page Street and you will find

Still another
Diane di Prima apartment   19.
263 Laguna

Just across from the Zen Center on Page Street is the apartment where di Prima lived for nearly two decades, from
1978 until 1995. As a practicing Buddhist and teacher at
the Zen Center, it was convenient for her. During the
1970s, she moved from political activism to a more serene
and meditative life. Amazingly productive during the
eighties and nineties, she published *Selected Poems
1956–1975* and *Loba,* cofounded the poetics faculty at the
New College of San Francisco in the Mission district,
worked with the San Francisco Institute of Magical and

Healing Arts, kept in touch with her kids, and traveled much with her partner, Sheppard Powell. Di Prima studied Tibetan Buddhism with Chögyam Trungpa Rinpoche until his death.

Turn around and walk one block north on Laguna past the Zen Center to

Bruce Conner's place 20.
400 Oak

Bruce Conner was one of the best San Francisco artists to get his start during the 1960s Renaissance. He exhibited in many of the avant-garde galleries in the city, including the Batman and Spatsa Galleries. He was a friend of Philip Lamantia, Michael McClure, and Jay DeFeo, and an image from one of his celebrated assemblages illustrated the cover of Lamantia's *Destroyed Works*. He is no doubt the most important of the San Francisco assemblage artists, a group fully documented in Rebecca Solnit's book, *Secret Exhibition*.

Turn left on Oak halfway up the block to

Jan Kerouac's apartment 21.
457 Oak

Just after the "Summer of Love" in 1968, Jan Kerouac moved into this little Victorian house. She was the daughter of Jack Kerouac and his second wife, Joan Haverty, but Jack never acknowledged that she was his. They met only twice in her life, but on their second meeting, when she was much older, he told her she could use his name, which she understood as his acceptance of her as his flesh and blood. Dark and beautiful, she was the spitting image of Jack, and there was no doubt whose daughter she was. One thing that Jan had in common with her father was an ability to write, and she published two autobiographical novels, *Baby Driver* and *Train Song*. On December 3, 1968, she married John Lash and began a nomadic existence often south of the border. She died young of kidney failure in 1996.

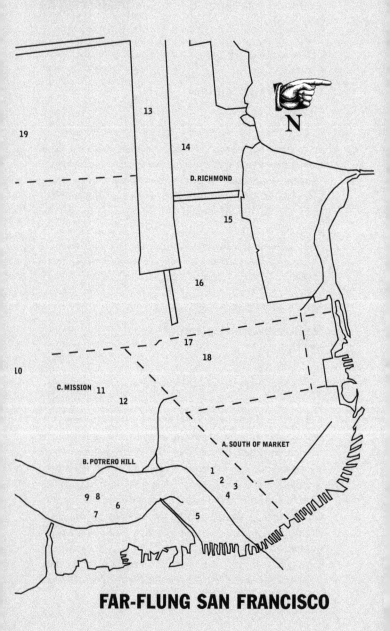

TOUR 10

13

19

14

D. RICHMOND

15

16

17

18

10

C. MISSION   11

12

A. SOUTH OF MARKET

B. POTRERO HILL

1

2   3

4

9 8

7   6

5

N

FAR-FLUNG SAN FRANCISCO

LAWRENCE FERLINGHETTI AND ALLEN GINSBERG AT 706 WISCONSIN STREET.
PHOTO BY ARTHUR STOCKETT, COURTESY OF JASMINE STOCKETT

FAR-FLUNG SAN FRANCISCO
South of Market, Potrero Hill, The Mission, Richmond, Sunset, and Park Merced

a. South of Market

You'll want to consider biking, driving, or taking public transportation on these tours, where there may be considerable distance between sites.

To a greater extent than even the Market Street corridor, South of Market (SOMA) has undergone radical change. The construction of the Moscone Convention Center, the baseball park, the Museum of Modern Art, and dot.com businesses spurred development and gentrification, with new live-work lofts, performance spaces, galleries, businesses, restaurants, and late-night clubs.

Start at Howard and Mary Streets, not far from Fifth Street.

Mime Troupe Loft   1.
924 Howard

In the early 1960s, Ronnie Davis, once an assistant director with the Actors Workshop, founded the San Francisco
Mime Troupe in an old Baptist church on Capp Street in
the Mission district. This was one of the very first guerril-
la theaters in the United States, and based on the
Commedia del Arte, with masks, period costumes, and fig-
ures who caricatured contemporary politicians, bosses,
and power brokers. The action satirized current political
issues on both local and international fronts, comically
castigating government and big business alike.

There were many spinoffs over the years from the early
San Francisco Mime Troupe, including Teatro Campesino,
directed by Luis Valdez (now still performing in San Juan
Bautista along the coast), who was an early Mime Troupe
member.

Ronnie Davis brought Bertolt Brecht's "alienation"
concepts to bear on Mime Troupe productions, with all
of Brecht's commitment to radical change and revolution,
performed with caustic satiric bravura. Soon after its
founding, the troupe rented the Calliope Warehouse, an
old horse and buggy stable, here at 924 Howard Street.
On November 6, 1965, Bill Graham staged a benefit and
the line of spectators stretched around the block to hear
Ferlinghetti, Ginsberg, the Fugs (a group of satiric musical poets), the first Jefferson Airplane (who practiced in
the Mime Troupe's loft), the Family Dog, the Warlocks,
guitarist Sandy Bull, and an improv group called the
Committee. The price of admission was set according to
the ability to pay; the unemployed were asked to donate
spare change; and the top tickets cost eighty-nine cents.
Bill Graham stood at the door, stuffing the cash into
cloth bags.

The following year this warehouse was the scene of
the notorious welcome-home party for Ken Kesey and
the Merry Pranksters, back from exile in Mexico, super-
ficially immortalized by Tom Wolfe in *The Electric
Kool-Aid Acid Test.*

*Go east on Howard one block to Fourth Street. On the northwest
corner is a new building, on what had been the site of the*

Mars Hotel 2.
192 Fourth Street

Another victim of the wrecker's ball was the hotel made famous by the Grateful Dead's 1974 album, *From the Mars Hotel*. Kerouac stayed here, and with Philip Whalen ended a very wild weekend. He recorded that Ferlinghetti had the hotel's desk clerk open the door "and what does he see but me out on the floor among bottles."

Continue one more block east on Howard, past the Moscone Convention Center, and turn right onto Third Street for two more blocks, and stop near the northeast corner of Harrison near the site of the

Cameo Hotel 3.
389 Third Street

Jack Kerouac's favorite hotel in the rundown train station district of the 1950s was the Cameo Hotel, then located here. (The whole block has recently been leveled and rebuilt.) He wrote the wonderful story "October in the Railroad Earth" and *San Francisco Blues* in his room at the Cameo, sitting "in a rockingchair at the window, looking down on winos and bebop winos and whores and cop cars." This was a fertile period for Jack, who was writing every day, and this neighborhood inspired passages in *On the Road* and *Desolation Angels* as well. Down the street at Third and Howard was what Kerouac considered the "wildest bar in America," and on the same corner was the Belfast Building, "the beatup tenement [that] has Belfast painted black on yellow on the side," but all that has now disappeared. Gone also is Little Harlem, once at 707 Folsom between Third and Fourth Streets, a crazy rhythm-and-blues bar that he wrote about in *On the Road*.

In *Lonesome Traveler*, Kerouac vividly described waking up in the Cameo Hotel and realizing that he was late for work. He had only three minutes to get from here to the station at Third and Townsend before his 7:15 train pulled out. "I start in a panic to job, goddam it I didn't give myself enough time this morning, I hurry down under the Harrison ramp to the Oakland-Bay Bridge, down past Schweibacker-Frey the great dim red neon printshop always spectrally my father the dead executive I see there,

THE BEAT GENERATION IN SAN FRANCISCO

I run and hurry past the beat Negro grocery stores where I buy all my peanut butter and raisin bread, past the red-brick railroad alley now mist and wet, across Townsend, the train is leaving!"

On that run down Third he would have passed the plaque on the building at 601–605 Third Street marking the site of Jack London's birth. Nearby is the recently named Jack London Street. In one poem from the same period, Kerouac wrote "Third Street Number 6-15 / Where Bank now stands / Jack London was born / And saw gray rigging / At the 'barcadero / Pier, His bier / commemorated in marble / To advertise the stone / Of vaults where money rots."

Continue south on Third Street underneath the Harrison ramp for two more blocks to the block past Brannan. Stop at

Rolling Stone Offices 4.
645 Third Street

Rolling Stone was founded in an old building that is still standing a few blocks away at 746 Brannan Street. On November 9, 1967, the first issue of the legendary rock newspaper, edited by Jann Wenner, was put together there at the peak of the rock revolution. As *Rolling Stone* grew, their offices moved here to Third Street, before leaving town completely.

Continue on Third Street to the corner of Townsend and turn right, stopping at the

Southern Pacific Depot 5.
Townsend and Fourth Street

The train station is now located on Fourth Street between King and Townsend. In Kerouac's day a Spanish Colonial–style Southern Pacific railroad station was located between Third and Fourth Streets. It has been replaced by the postmodern glass shed you find here today. Cassady was working on the Southern Pacific in the late 1940s. He persuaded Jack Kerouac to come out west and helped him get a job as a baggage handler and yard clerk in 1951 and then as a brakeman in 1952. A few years later, Allen Ginsberg applied for a job here, too, but he wasn't at all suited for manual labor and it never worked out for him. Kerouac wrote about his railroad days in several books and most notably in his greatest short story, "October in the Railroad Earth." Ginsberg wrote of his vision of the life force in the poem "Sunflower Sutra" after Jack had pointed out he'd seen a battered, dying sunflower along the tracks south of the station. "I rushed up enchanted—it was my first sunflower, memories of Blake—my visions— . . ." Parking lots now cover that same area.

b. Potrero Hill

If you want to walk, be forewarned that it is a long way. If you take the bus, transfer at 18th Street to the bus that climbs Potrero Hill over the bridge. If you walk, go out Fourth Street to the intersection with Third, bearing to the right onto Third, continue south to 18th Street, then turn right across the bridge to Potrero Hill. Turn onto the second street on your left after crossing the bridge. That street is Mississippi and after almost two blocks you will see

Richard Brautigan's apartment 6.
461 Mississippi

This three-story building is where Richard Brautigan lived with his wife Virginia, around 1959. Brautigan was born in Tacoma, Washington, in 1935, and came to San Francisco when he was nineteen. He liked the Beats, but his whimsical writing was very different from theirs and it didn't become popular until the 1960s, when his droll humor made a hit with the new generation of flower children. Michael McClure noted that "Richard always dressed the same. It was his style and he wanted to change it as little as possible. Richard's style was shabby —loose threads at the cuff, black pants faded to gray, an old mismatched vest, a navy pea jacket, and later something like love beads around his neck. As he began to be successful he was even more fearful of change." Richard and Virginia had one daughter, Ianthe, born in 1960, who would later write a biographical memoir of her father, called *You Can't Catch Death*.

Continue south just a few houses and turn right onto 20th Street for two blocks to Missouri. Turn left on Missouri and go down the hill and then up the hill to the projects, bearing left onto the first street to

LAFCADIO AND PETER ORLOVSKY AT 5 TURNER TERRACE, 1956.
©2002 ALLEN GINSBERG TRUST

Peter Orlovsky's apartment 7.
5 Turner Terrace

In February 1956, after living with Allen Ginsberg in
North Beach for several months, Peter Orlovsky moved
with his brother Lafcadio to an apartment of his own in
the projects, which are still standing at 5 Turner Terrace.
The bunkerlike housing unit is over the hill on the left as
you enter Turner Terrace. Kerouac wrote about Orlovsky's
pad in *Desolation Angels,* "where you see the giant gas-
tanks of eternity and a whole vista of the smoky industrial Frisco including the bay and the railroad mainline and
factories." The houses were built in 1940 for workers in
the naval shipyards at nearby Hunter's Point and converted to low-income housing after the war. Orlovsky and

ALLEN GINSBERG AT THE TYPEWRITER, 5 TURNER TERRACE.
PHOTO © ALLEN GINSBERG TRUST

Ginsberg walked back and forth between downtown and Potrero Hill along Third Street to see each other. Ginsberg recalls his impression of the area, "Walking up the Potrero hill against moving scenery of industrial landscape last night, thought of Whitman's line '. . . is enough to stagger sextillions of infidels'—and looked at the telephone pole, hoping to be staggered, and was by the uprearing brown raw wooden tree raised instantaneously by outside intelligence to stand there propped up dumb holding up the wires . . ."

Retrace your steps down Missouri and then back up to 20th Street. Turn left and walk for three blocks to Wisconsin and turn left again. Up the hill you will find

Kenneth Rexroth's house 8.
692 Wisconsin

From the day Rexroth arrived in San Francisco in 1927, he was *the* literary authority and he became the main mover in the San Francisco Renaissance. (He claimed to have arrived in San Francisco the very day poet George Sterling killed himself and thus naturally inherited the mantle of the elder poet.)

This is the two-story frame house where he lived with his second wife, Marie Kass, from 1935 until 1947 when they moved to the Richmond district, to be closer to Marie's mother. It was here that Rexroth initiated his liter-

Photo by Bill Morgan

ary Friday nights, where poets, Wobblies, and intellectuals of every stripe shot the bull for hours. A commanding presence, he had a gift for the burlesque and exercised a caustic and sometimes affectionate wit. Here he wrote his first book of poetry, *In What Hour*, published in 1941. In 1942 when Henry Miller first came to California, he stayed with the Rexroths before settling in Big Sur.

Two doors up the hill is

Lawrence Ferlinghetti's house 9.
706 Wisconsin

Lawrence Ferlinghetti bought this Victorian in 1958. It was in bad condition and didn't cost much, partly because the working-class neighborhood was permeated with rank smells from the slaughterhouses down the hill on Third Street. When he wasn't working on the house, Ferlinghetti wrote in the attic on two large tables with windows overlooking the city and the inner bay. In one poem he wrote here, he said, "Dreaming of utopias / where everyone's a lover / I see San Francisco from my window / through some old navy beerbottles . . ."

He would work at his typewriter in the mornings and then go to City Lights Bookstore, with his dog Homer, for the rest of the day. Ferlinghetti said that the front end of the dog was collie, the chassis poodle, and the rear end cocker—in other words, a "Cockapoolie."

Julie and Lorenzo Ferlinghetti, Lawrence and Kirby's two children, were born in 1961 and 1962. The family lived here until 1972, when Lawrence moved to an apartment back in North Beach. Visitors to the house in the high Beat years were Kerouac, Ginsberg, Cassady, Orlovsky, "Lord and Lady" Buckley, and William Saroyan. Jerry Kamstra, the author of *The Frisco Kid,* lived in the basement apartment for a few years. The neighborhood is very upscale now and the slaughterhouses are gone, but the house is much the same as when Ferlinghetti lived and wrote here.

From this point you can take the number 48 bus to the Mission district. Then change on Mission Street to another bus out to 30th Street.

c. The Mission

Head west on 30th Street for three blocks and after crossing Sanchez Street look for Sanchez Street again on the left. Go up the hill a few houses to

Philip Lamantia's birthplace   10.
1715 Sanchez

Poet Philip Lamantia was born in an upstairs bedroom in the light-grayish-green bungalow near the bottom of this steep hill on October 23, 1927. He was the son of Sicilian immigrants, Nunzio and Mary Tarantino Lamantia. Lamantia remembered the early influence of his paternal grandmother, who told him spellbinding folktales of her native Sicily. After attending Longfellow Elementary School, he began writing poetry in junior high school. He was first published in 1942 and went to New York to begin the free-spirited life of a poet. On returning to San Francisco a couple of years later, he got his high school equivalency and took classes at UC Berkeley. His family moved to the Excelsior district and when Lamantia's Beat

PHILIP LAMANTIA, 1956. PHOTO BY GOLDIAN NESBIT

poet friends were in town, his mother was always happy to invite "the boys with good healthy appetites" to come over for an enormous Italian feast. At the Six Gallery reading, he read poems by John Hoffman, a friend who had died young in Mexico. After many years in Mexico and Europe, with sporadic stays in San Francisco, he settled in North Beach in 1968, where he has lived ever since.

Go back down Sanchez to 30th Street and continue east to Church Street, then turn north on Church for eighteen blocks, almost a mile, to Liberty Street and turn right to

Carolyn Cassady's apartment 11.
109 Liberty

On December 15, 1948, Neal Cassady left Carolyn with their new baby and drove his friends, Al and Helen Hinkle, to Denver, and then continued on to the East Coast. But this wasn't just another of his many cross-country trips. It's the trip Kerouac records in *On the Road.* When he returned to San Francisco around the first of February 1949, he brought Kerouac with him. By that time, Carolyn had moved to 109 Liberty Street, where all three, Neal, Carolyn, and Jack, lived together. In *On the Road* Jack Kerouac describes this apartment and nearby Mission Dolores Park.

Continue east on Liberty Street one more block to Valencia, stopping at the

Abandoned Planet Bookstore 12.
518 Valencia

Poet Jack Micheline was often in this bookstore. He, along with Gregory Corso and Bob Kaufman, are often thought of as the only members of the Beat Generation who were truly "Beat," in the sense that they lived marginally, as self-educated street poets. Micheline was born in the Bronx in 1929 as Harvey Silver, and changed his name evidently to distance himself from his father. He came to public attention when Jack Kerouac wrote an introduction for his 1958 book of poems, *River of Red Wine.* After it was reviewed favorably in *Esquire* magazine by none other than Dorothy Parker, Micheline became a literary nova. Years later he settled in San Francisco, living in funky

JACK MICHELINE IN THE MISSION. PHOTO BY CHRISTOPHER FELVER

hotels and rooming houses in North Beach, and finally in the Mission district. In 1995, the owner of the Abandoned Planet Bookstore suggested that Micheline paint a mural on the wall in the back room and he proceeded to cover the entire room with populist-expressionist murals. Micheline never really was recognized for the cool poet and painter he was until the very last years of his life when *Ragged Lion: A Tribute to Jack Micheline,* edited by John Bennett, was published.

d: Richmond, Sunset, and ParkMerced

Polo Field   13.
Golden Gate Park near the
30th Avenue entrance to the park

One of the defining events of the 1960s took place at the Polo Field on January 14, 1967. According to various esti-

mates, between 20,000 and 100,000 romantics and ideal-
ists celebrated the flowering of the counterculture with
Edenic musing and ecstatic dancing and chanting, led by
Timothy Leary, Allen Ginsberg, and Gary Snyder, among
others. This was announced as a "gathering of the tribes,"
the First Human Be-In. The *San Francisco Oracle* proph-
esied: "A union of love and activism previously separated
by categorical dogma and label mongering will finally
occur ecstatically when Berkeley political activists and hip
community and San Francisco's spiritual generation and
contingents from the emerging revolutionary generation
all over California meet." At this preview of the "Summer
of Love," with a new spirit of hope for the future, the poets
performed, the great rock bands played, and Leary urged
the crowd to "turn on to the scene, tune in to what is happening, and drop out." This marked the high point of the
Haight-Ashbury scene, when it was still young and beautiful, before its sad decline into heavier drugs and lost
youths with dead eyes.

Carolyn Cassady's house   14.
561A 24th Avenue (between Geary and Anza)

In 1947, Carolyn Robinson lived here when she first began
seeing Neal Cassady. In *Off the Road,* she describes the
events that led to their wedding in 1948 and chronicles
their tumultuous life together when she was still filled
with hopes for a traditional marriage.

Here Neal tried his hand at writing prose for the first
time and in a letter to Ginsberg said, "I am stumbling thru
a daily journal and try as I might am having trouble with
the recollections of my early life. This first writing task
will be all the more difficult in that I do it daily (everyday
thought)." The final result was Neal's only book, the autobiographical *The First Third.*

Kenneth Rexroth's apartment   15.
187 Eighth Avenue (on the corner of California)

In December 1947, Kenneth Rexroth and his wife Marie
rented a flat in this large three-story house. Kenneth and
Marie had lived for twelve years on Potrero Hill and now
their relationship was nearly over. Kenneth began seeing

Marthe Larsen shortly after the move here. The erudite Rexroth continued his Friday night open house, which many poets attended. Shortly after the Six Gallery reading, Rexroth invited Ginsberg, Kerouac, Snyder, and Whalen for dinner. The younger poets, already exuberantly high by the time they arrived, were not in a mood to be respectful, and the dinner was a disaster. Rexroth wanted to give guidance and advice, but they would have none of it. Arguments escalated until Kerouac called Rexroth a *Boche* [a derogatory French name for the Germans] and Ginsberg loudly boasted that he was a better poet than Rexroth. Rexroth kicked them out, and as they retreated, Kerouac continued to shout back, "Dirty German!" As time went on Rexroth became openly hostile toward the Beats for various reasons; he even broke with some of them altogether, although he continued to appreciate much of their work.

University of San Francisco   16.
2800 Turk (west of Masonic)

In the summer of 1952, Lawrence Ferlinghetti taught a class in Shakespeare at this Jesuit-run university. After the head of the department discovered him lecturing on "The Homosexual Interpretation of Shakespeare's *Sonnets,*" he was not invited back the following term. Times have changed, for Ferlinghetti is now a Fellow of the university's Gleason Library and his lecture notes are a part of the library's rare book and manuscript collection. The library also owns a draft of Neal Cassady's manuscript of *The First Third.*

Michael and Joanna McClure's flat   17.
707 Scott (near Grove on Alamo Square)

Alamo Square is one of the most photographed places in San Francisco; the spectacular panorama of the city skyline above nearby Victorian houses makes a great postcard. In the fifties, Michael and Joanna McClure shared the house at 707 Scott with Jim and Beverly Harmon, Ronnie Bladen, and a few other friends. In 1956 they set up a press in the basement and published an anarchist little magazine called *Ark II, Moby I,* with contributions by Robert Creeley, Ed Dorn, Robert Duncan, Richard

Eberhart, Lawrence Ferlinghetti, Allen Ginsberg, Jack
Kerouac, Denise Levertov, Charles Olson, Kenneth
Patchen, Kenneth Rexroth, Gary Snyder, Philip Whalen,
William Carlos Williams, and Louis Zukofsky. John
Wieners wrote his own journal in that house with the
awkward title *The Journal of John Wieners Is to Be Called
707 Scott Street for Billie Holiday 1959.*

The Libertarian Circle 18.
1057 Steiner (on the corner of Golden Gate)

The huge, ornate Victorian on the southwest corner of
Golden Gate and Steiner is now the Chateau Tivoli Bed
and Breakfast, but in the 1940s this was the more altruis-
tic Workman's Circle, or "Arbeiter Ring." The Libertarian
Circle of philosophical anarchists was formed within the
IWW union (Wobblies) after the Sacco and Vanzetti trials.
Their meetings sometimes swelled, especially when a
topic like "Sex and Anarchy" was announced. Robert
Duncan, Philip Lamantia, Richard Moore, and Kenneth
Rexroth were early literary members and in 1946 they
established the Poetry Forum, meeting every Wednesday.
Rexroth acted as semi-official leader and provided read-
ing lists. William Everson, Thomas Parkinson, Muriel
Rukeyser, and Jack Spicer also took part. The *Ark,* an
anarchist little magazine, grew out of these meetings.

San Francisco State University
and the Poetry Center 19.
1600 Holloway (at 19th)

The Poetry Center at San Francisco State University has
one of the largest and most comprehensive archives of
tape and video recordings of contemporary poetry in the
world. Ruth Witt-Diamant, an English professor here
since the 1930s, found financial backing for audio record-
ings of early readings organized by Kenneth Rexroth and
Madeline Gleason. Out of this the Poetry Center was born.
W. H. Auden dedicated the Poetry Center with Witt-
Diamant in 1954. He spoke on "The Hero in Modern
Literature." Madeline Gleason founded the San Francisco
Poetry Guild, and in 1959–60 she led a workshop at the
Poetry Center. Her assistant was Robert Duncan, who

ALLEN GINSBERG READING AT THE POETRY CENTER, 1955. PHOTO BY RUTH WITT- DIAMANT

recruited fresh talent. Since that time, scores of poets have read and recorded at the center. Dylan Thomas was the greatest to read there in the 1950s, but the list included most of the important American avant-garde of the period.

Allen Ginsberg gave one of his earliest readings at the center on November 20, 1955, just a few weeks after the Six Gallery reading. Ginsberg remembered that Witt-Diamant "asked me not to say any of the 'dirty words,' because she was afraid she'd get busted or it would create a scandal for the Poetry Center." As a result, his reading wasn't very relaxed and he substituted the word "censored" for the actual words in the poem. The recording was later released as a commercial album.

In 1956, William Everson gave his first public reading as Brother Antoninus at the Poetry Center. The local press called him a "Beat Priest," and soon the archbishop of San Francisco forbid him to read in public. A lay brother in the Dominicans, Antoninus passed agonizing years in conflict between his religious vocation and his calling as a poet, and sometime toward the end of the 1960s he finally threw off his robes and went to live in Stinson Beach with Susanna Dickson, a young woman who had originally come to him for spiritual counseling. They were later married. Everson became a university lecturer and master printer at the Lime Kiln Press at the University of California at Santa Cruz. He died in 1994.

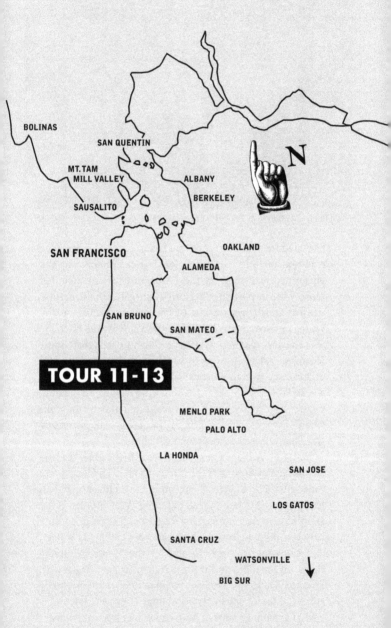

BOLINAS

SAN QUENTIN

MT. TAM
MILL VALLEY

SAUSALITO

ALBANY

BERKELEY

N

SAN FRANCISCO

OAKLAND

ALAMEDA

SAN BRUNO

SAN MATEO

TOUR 11-13

MENLO PARK

PALO ALTO

LA HONDA

SAN JOSE

LOS GATOS

SANTA CRUZ

WATSONVILLE

BIG SUR

ALLEN GINSBERG ON DURANT STREET IN BERKELEY, NEAR KIP'S,
MID-1950S. PHOTO © ALLEN GINSBERG TRUST

EAST BAY TOUR

Albany

Golden Gate Fields Racetrack   1.
(Off I-80 just north of Berkeley)

This track, "Where the Bay Comes to Play," is where Neal
Cassady played the ponies and tried his luck with one
new "system" after another. In both *On the Road* and
Desolation Angels Kerouac wrote about Golden Gate
Fields. In the latter, he records one occasion on which
Cassady won $40 and Corso came out even. Kerouac
himself didn't bet, instead calling the track "an ant-heap
in Nirvana."

Oaks Theater   2.
1875 Solano (at The Alameda)

In May 1957, Jack Kerouac went to see a double feature
here: *Thunder in the Sun* and *Tokyo after Dark*. He
described the view when he emerged from the theater.
". . . and just as I step out of the theater at midnight I
look down the street towards San Francisco Bay completely forgetting where I am and I see the Golden Gate

Bridge shining in the night, and I *shudder with horror*. The bottom drops out of my soul."

Berkeley

Thomas Parkinson's house 3.
1001 Cragmont

One of the earliest academics to write serious, scholarly evaluations of Beat literature was Thomas Parkinson, whose *Casebook on the Beats* is the earliest critical appreciation of it. Parkinson was a crucial witness for the defense at the "Howl" trial. He was later shot in the face by a crazed student who burst into his office with a shotgun. The scattered shot disfigured Parkinson for life.

Jaime de Angulo's house 4.
2845 Buena Vista Way

Jaime de Angulo's Maybeck-designed home here, which overlooks Berkeley and the entire San Francisco Bay, was in the 1930s and 1940s, a lively gathering place for bohemians and intellectuals. Angulo was a maverick genius who gave inspiration to the Berkeley and San Francisco Renaissances without really being a part of them. He had a medical degree, but his real interest was in anthropology and linguistics. By the time Robert Duncan met him in 1948, Angulo had already mastered seventeen different Native American languages. On the suggestion of Ezra Pound, Duncan sought work with Angulo as live-in secretary and he helped assemble his papers for publication. Later, the house was the home of his daughter, painter Gui de Angulo, who wrote two biographical memoirs about him. Jack Kerouac wrote about him and Gui in *Desolation Angels*.

Allen Ginsberg's cottage 5.
1624 Milvia Street

In September 1955, shortly after writing "Howl," Allen Ginsberg moved to a little cottage here, which rented for only $35 a month. It stood in the backyard of some larger houses. New apartment buildings have replaced all those buildings now. It was a perfect residence for Ginsberg,

ALLEN GINSBERG POSING AS "ST FRANCIS IN ECSTASY" BY BELLINI, IN THE
BACKYARD OF HIS COTTAGE IN BERKELEY.   PHOTO © ALLEN GINSBERG TRUST

who was writing poetry, trying to straighten out his relationship with Peter Orlovsky, and thinking about going
back to school at Berkeley for a Master's degree. He was
living here when he first read "Howl" at the Six Gallery
in San Francisco in October. His poem, "A Strange New
Cottage in Berkeley," immortalized the place. In his journal Ginsberg noted, "home midnite to pancakes high &
Jupiter Symphony & garden & moonlight & loneliness—The huge horror of Berkeley ahead—could be
nice, but ugly forebodings all day, job worry & study
fears & the million books of scholars unreadable."
Ginsberg also noted that he studiously reread Whitman's
Leaves of Grass here.

Jack Kerouac described the cottage in *The Dharma
Bums*. "In Berkeley I was living with Alvah Goldbook
[Ginsberg] in his little rose-covered cottage in the backyard of a bigger house on Milvia Street. The old rotten
porch slanted forward to the ground, among vines, with
a nice old rocking chair that I sat in every morning to
read my Diamond Sutra . . ." He also mentioned
Ginsberg's Bach records and phonograph loud enough
"to blast the roof off."

Ginsberg learned here that his mother, Naomi, had died
in a mental hospital in New York. He would later write his

greatest poem, "Kaddish," in her memory. In June 1956, Ginsberg gave up the cottage to Philip Whalen. In 1999 "The Allen Ginsberg Poetry Garden" was dedicated in the front yard of the school directly across the street.

Augustus Owsley Stanley III's house   6.
1647 Virginia Street (on the corner of McGee)

Augustus Owsley Stanley III (or just Owsley, as he was known) became the most famous producer of LSD in California during the 1960s, setting up his first acid lab in this little house. After he was busted in 1965, authorities were embarrassed to find that he hadn't broken any laws, and he was released. (Until October 1966 there were no laws against LSD in California.) Owsley soon moved his operations to the more lucrative Los Angeles. The main supplier for Ken Kesey's Merry Pranksters as described in Tom Wolfe's *Electric Kool-Aid Acid Test,* his name became synonymous with a high-quality product.

Robert Duncan's apartment   7.
2029 Hearst

In 1946 Duncan moved into a three-room apartment on the first floor of this house, where he started a kind of bohemian collective, "The New Athens." The lacquered round table in the dining room became the fulcrum of the Berkeley Renaissance; around it the poets discussed literature, performed plays by Shakespeare and Stein, and conducted magic and occult experiments. While living here in 1947, Duncan published his first collection of poetry *Heavenly City, Earthly City.*

Jack Kerouac's apartment   8.
1943 Berkeley Way (between
Martin Luther King Jr. Way and Milvia)

Jack Kerouac talked his mother into moving to California in 1957, just before the publication of *On the Road.* Here Jack found a ground-floor apartment with a garden. (It's been torn down to make way for the large building that now takes up most of the block.) They didn't stay long.

The day before they left Berkeley, in mid-July 1957, advance copies of *On the Road* arrived from Viking Press.

Kerouac didn't want to give away all his author's copies, but Neal persuaded him to open the box and pass out books to one and all. Then Jack and Neal and friends headed over the bridge to San Francisco to celebrate.

Original KPFA/ FM studios 9.
2054 University Avenue
(between Shattuck and Milvia)

In the early 1950s, the small listener-supported radio station KPFA Pacifica became the intellectual center of the Bay Area. Until very recently the broadcast studios were in the Koeber Building here. KPFA was founded in 1949 by anarchist-pacifist Lewis Hill and was from the start one of the greatest supporters of avant-garde writing in the country. The station's celebrated literature programs brought great writing and live interviews with writers to a vast radio audience. All the Beat writers were recorded at the station, some of them creating original works for radio. Today, a project has begun to preserve invaluable archival tapes.

Robert Duncan's apartment 10.
2018 McKinley (now demolished)

In late 1947 Duncan moved from Hearst Street to share an apartment here with Jerry Ackerman. The two had a brief, tempestuous relationship filled with arguments, separations, and reconciliations. During one of these separations, Duncan sat alone for three days and wrote one of his best poems, "Venice Poem."

Philip Lamantia also lived in this house for a short period, and next door lived the science fiction writer Philip K. Dick, who worked in a Berkeley record store, owned a sophisticated sound system, and recorded all the neighborhood poets.

Larry Eigner's house 11.
2338 McGee Street (near the corner of Channing Way)

Poet Larry Eigner was born on August 7, 1927, in Swampscott, Massachusetts. From infancy Eigner suffered from cerebral palsy and was confined to a wheelchair, but that didn't stop him from taking a serious interest in liter-

ature. In 1978 he moved to Berkeley to live with his brother, Richard, and wrote several books while living in this
small dark brown Swiss-looking house, including most of
the poems included in *Areas Lights Heights*. One of the
last he published was: "September 16 92 / so years been
passing / the road quiet / still often enough / night and
then day / light up in the sky / behind a towering tree /
shadowed dense." Eigner died of pneumonia in the Alta
Bates Hospital in Berkeley on February 3, 1996.

University of California at Berkeley   12.
Bancroft Way and Telegraph Avenue

Sather Gate is a main entrance to the campus just north
of Telegraph Avenue. While living in Berkeley in 1955
Ginsberg wrote in his "Sather Gate Illumination": ". . .The
Campanile pokes its white granite (?) innocent head into
the clouds for me to look at . . . And do you know that all
these rubbings of the eyes & painful gestures to the brow
of suited scholars entering Dwinelle (Hall) are Holy
Signs? —anxiety and fear? . . . And there goes Professor
Hart striding enlightened by the years through the doorway and arcade he built (in his mind) and knows—he too
saw the ruins of Yucatán once . . ." Sather Gate was to be
the focal point of the Free Speech Movement and the student revolts of the late 1960s in the era of anti–Vietnam
War protests.

The university's Bancroft Library has one of the most
important literary collections in the world, including a
treasure trove of materials related to Berkeley and San
Francisco Renaissances and the Beat Generation. There
are the City Lights and Lawrence Ferlinghetti archives, the
papers of Dave Haselwood and the Auerhahn Press, and
archives of Richard Brautigan, Phillip Whalen, Michael
McClure, and David Meltzer.

Kip's Restaurant   13.
2439 Durant Avenue (just west of Telegraph)

Since 1954 Kip's Restaurant has been a place where
Berkeley students could sit around studying and talking.
Shortly after it opened, Allen Ginsberg got a job here as a
busboy, but he never could hold down a regular job, and

this was no exception. After just a week or two he was fired. In his journal he wrote, "So Mrs. Robinson's final excuse when firing me from busboy job at Kips Restaurant, Berkeley—'The work is too much for you.' It was too much for her, that's why she thought to say that to me, to change the situation." Allen had his picture taken here on Durant Avenue at about the same time.

Robert Duncan's house 14.
2643 Telegraph Avenue
(at the corner of Derby Street)

Unfortunately, the Victorian mansion known as "Throckmorton Manor" where Robert Duncan lived and first organized his antiuniversity seminars in 1946 is now replaced by a supermarket.

Ann Charters's cottage 15.
2803 1/2 Forest Avenue
(near the corner of Piedmont)

When Jack Kerouac's first biographer, Ann Charters, was a student at Berkeley from 1953 to 1957, she moved out of the dorms and into this cottage her senior year. She remembers it as "one of the ramshackle, poorly insulated, small wooden buildings scattered throughout the city, usually tucked away in the tree shaded backyard gardens behind larger houses." Her first meeting with Kerouac led her into a career as a leading scholar of Beat literature.

Gary Snyder's cottage 16.
2919 Hillegass Street (north of Ashby)

The cottage Gary Snyder lived in was just a gardener's tool shed in 1955 and his living conditions were Spartan. Today, it has been fixed up as a proper student apartment, according to Snyder. Back then, it was just twelve foot square, with no furniture, straw mats covering the floor, and fruit-crate bookcases. He used camping utensils to cook his meals over a small hibachi. Kerouac had heard so much about Snyder that he hurried over to meet him and described Snyder as "a happy little sage." In 1953 Gary Snyder entered the East Asian languages program at the

GARY SNYDER IN HIS BACKYARD HUT, BERKELEY.   PHOTO © ALLEN GINSBERG TRUST

university and attended regularly until 1956, when he left to study in Japan. He stayed there for a decade, eventually taking formal Buddhist vows from Roshi Oda Sesso, and has been a practicing Buddhist ever since.

At Kenneth Rexroth's suggestion, Ginsberg walked over to meet Gary Snyder at his cottage, and learned much from him about Buddhism, meditation, Asian languages, and ecology.

Town Hall Theater (now the Berkeley Cafe and Bowling Alley)   17. Shattuck Avenue and Stuart Street

The landmark reading at the Six Gallery was reenacted here five months later, on March 18, 1956. It was the first time that Ginsberg read the complete finished text of "Howl," which was still in rough form at the Six Gallery reading. The evening here was a much more theatrical event than the one at the Six Gallery. Rexroth was dressed in a cutaway tuxedo with a black turtleneck sweater from the Salvation Army. The only poet who read at the Six Gallery who missed this reading was Philip Lamantia, who was in Mexico staying with the Cora Indians at the time.

Alameda

Robert Duncan's boyhood home   18.
1700 Pearl Street (at Buena Vista)

Robert Duncan was raised in this tiny suburban house. He was born in Oakland on January 7, 1919, but when his mother died in childbirth his father put him up for adoption and he was raised in the home of Edwin Joseph Symmes and Minnehaha Harris. His stepfather, Symmes, had designed the house himself. Later the family moved to Bakersfield when Robert was eight years old. He attended UC Berkeley but dropped out before graduation. Although he enrolled under the name Robert Symmes, he later took back his birth name, Duncan.

After a brief stay on the East Coast in 1946, he returned to Berkeley, where a literary movement formed around him, as one had formed around Kenneth Rexroth across the bay in San Francisco.

ROBERT DUNCAN. PHOTO BY RUTH WITT-DIAMANT

When Duncan moved permanently to San Francisco, the Berkeley and San Francisco Renaissances became one. Connections with the soon-to-arrive Beat Generation were vague at best until then. When the New York Beats reached San Francisco in the late 1940s and early 1950s, friendships were formed between the very different East and West Coast poets and San Francisco literary culture was permanently transformed.

TOUR 12

SOUTH BAY TOUR

San Bruno

Tanforan Race Track (demolished; now Tanforan Park Shopping Center)   1. I-380, El Camino Real exit

Tanforan was another of Neal Cassady's favorite tracks. Ginsberg describes a day at the races in his journal, ". . . where Neal Peter & I sit, Neal in middle, saying, everybody here has got his own idea about what's happening so you don't pay no attention to them, except a few people you notice or know—But I notice the lineup as in the great ramp to heaven, the lineup of worried faces, humans, with hats & raincoats folding papers, the slot into the sky with them all silhouetted, staring down on the great racetrack of illusion." Inspired by this vision, Ginsberg began to write his great "Holy! Holy! Holy! . . . The world is holy, the soul is holy" section of "Howl."

Ken Kesey describes a trip to the track with Cassady: "There was one incident in particular when he truly impressed me not only as a madman, genius, and poet but also as an avatar—someone in contact with other powers." Neal never slowed down for a single moment: "He was driving and talking very fast, checking his watch frantically, hoping we would get to the track on time. If we got to the track just before the last three races, we'd get in free. We made it just in time, and we bet on the last two races. Cassady had a theory about betting he'd learned in jail from someone named Knee-Walking Jackson. His theory was that the third favorite at post time is often the horse most likely to upset the winner and make big money. Cassady's strategy was to step up to the tellers at the ticket booths just at post time. He'd glance up to see who was third favorite and put money on that horse." Alas, the nags seldom cooperated in his strategy.

San Mateo

Bay Meadows Race Track 2.
El Camino Real exit off route 92

One day, certain that he'd picked the right horse, Neal asked his girlfriend, Natalie Jackson, to forge his wife Carolyn's name at the bank so he could "borrow" $10,000 from their joint account to make their fortune. But luck wasn't with him and he lost all of the loot that day at this track. Jack Kerouac wrote about Bay Meadows, "In San Francisco, city of enlightenment and culture and good manners, people go to the races to be seen in the latest fashions and to lose all their money. It is a shallow place."

La Honda

Ken Kesey's house 3.
Route 84

Evicted from his cottage in Palo Alto, Ken Kesey found a picturesque log house in the forest at La Honda, where he hoped he and his band of Merry Pranksters could avoid the attention of the police. Here he finished his second and best novel, *Sometimes a Great Notion*. After the 1964 pub-

KEN KESEY'S LOG HOUSE IN LA HONDA. PHOTO BY BILL MORGAN

lication of the book, Kesey gave up writing, saying, "I'd rather be a lightning rod than a seismograph." Neal Cassady had been spending a lot of time at La Honda and Kesey began to consider him a living book. "He did everything a novel does, except that he did it better because he was living it and not writing about it."

Kesey and his Merry Pranksters customized an old 1939 International Harvester school bus and decorated it in psychedelic colors with signs like "Further" and "Caution: Weird Load." Then they drove around the country high on LSD and filmed their mind-blown escapades and the public's reactions.

In 1964, Hunter S. Thompson introduced Kesey to the Hell's Angels and invited them to a big party at the La Honda house. At first it looked like the hippies and bikers might not get along, but soon they all got into the spirit of a wild two-day blast. Allen Ginsberg was there and wrote about it in his poem, "First Party at Ken Kesey's with Hells Angels." Ferlinghetti says he saw Kesey as "the Paul Bunyan of the Beat Generation." On April 23, 1965, Kesey and Page Browning were busted on marijuana charges. This was Kesey's first arrest, but he was arrested again just a few weeks later and fled to Mexico to avoid prosecution.

Tom Wolfe also described the La Honda scene in *The Electric Kool-Aid Acid Test*. The cops were all set to raid La Honda, but since LSD was legal at the time, they had to sit in their patrol cars across the creek and hope for trouble to break out. Later, after Kesey was convicted on drug charges, he had to sell the house as a condition for parole. He decided to move back to Oregon permanently. The house has been restored and raised on piers to avoid the periodic floods that swamped the cabin in the past. It is now a private residence, so please don't cross the bridge and bug the tenants with merry pranks.

Menlo Park

Veterans Administration Medical Center 4.
795 Willow Road

In 1961 Ken Kesey came here, not as a patient, but voluntarily as a human guinea pig. He was paid $20 a session to take a wide variety of experimental and psychedelic drugs. He told *Paris Review* editor George Plimpton, "I was taking mescaline and LSD. It gave me a different perspective on the people in the mental hospital, a sense that maybe they were not so crazy or as bad as the sterile environment they were living in. But psychedelics are only keys to worlds that are already there." Kesey also worked the all-night shift as an attendant in the mental ward and met the patients who inspired him to write his first book, *One Flew Over the Cuckoo's Nest.* Like the classic old film, *King of Hearts,* the characters of Kesey's story showed themselves to be not as mad as their keepers or as the outside world.

Palo Alto

Stanford University 5.

Many writers, from John Steinbeck to Yvor Winters to Ken Kesey, have been connected with Stanford, for better or for worse. It has some links with the Beat Generation and is an important research center for Beat studies today, having purchased the voluminous Ginsberg archive in 1994.

Ginsberg first took LSD in the mid-1950s, in a Stanford program to study the effects of new drugs on the human brain. The program was secretly funded by the military to explore the value of such drugs in warfare; however, these experiments also led directly to the mind-expanding culture of the 1960s.

Ken Kesey won a Woodrow Wilson Fellowship to Stanford University in 1958 at the age of twenty-four. He studied under Wallace Stegner, who had founded the creative writing program in 1947. But Stegner never did like Kesey and complained that he was uneducable. Kesey had another explanation: "I liked acid, while Stegner preferred Jack Daniels." Kesey got along better with another professor, Malcolm Cowley, and said that it was Cowley who taught him to respect other writers' feelings. In 1956 Jack Kerouac came to Palo Alto to work with Cowley, who was editing the manuscript of *On the Road* for Viking.

In addition to the mammoth Allen Ginsberg archive, the Special Collections Department at the university library houses the papers of Gregory Corso, Robert Creeley, Denise Levertov, Larry Eigner, Ron Loewinsohn, and Gil Sorrentino.

Ken Kesey's house 6.
Perry Lane

When Ken Kesey arrived with his new bride, Faye Haxby, from a small town in Oregon, they found a cozy little two-room cottage in the bohemian cluster known as Perry Lane. There are a few of these houses left, although not Kesey's. They give a good idea of what they were like. Built as emergency housing during World War I, they quartered soldiers in basic training. Taken over by artists, writers, and students after the war, Perry Lane became a free-thinking intellectual community where everyone knew everyone.

Kesey first met Neal Cassady here in the early sixties when Neal appeared from out of nowhere in Ken's driveway. Kesey said he never found out what had brought Cassady there; Cassady just announced that his Jeep had blown its transmission, and he began tearing the car apart, talking nonstop. ". . . that was one of my earliest impressions of him as I watched him running around, this frenetic, crazed character speaking in a monologue that sounded like *Finnegans Wake* played fast forward." Cassady and Kesey became buddies, and Neal drove the

Merry Pranksters' bus *Further* around the country for several years. Ken nicknamed Neal "Speed Limit," as much for his fast conversation as for his fast driving. Thus Kesey replaced Kerouac as Cassady's traveling buddy, after Kerouac retreated from Beat life, and faded from the scene.

Malcolm Cowley's house   7.
490 Oregon Avenue

When Malcolm Cowley accepted *On the Road* for Viking Press, Kerouac made plans to visit him here and work on revisions to the manuscript. Kerouac brought it to Cowley in the form of a huge scroll, just one long sheet of art paper typed without paragraph or chapter breaks. Cowley suggested to Kerouac that he retype it in page format because he knew that no publisher would ever look at it seriously in that form. Reluctantly Jack complied. Cowley also had reservations as to whether Kerouac could legally publish a work that so clearly depicted living people. In the end Jack was able to get releases from all of them, and plans for publication continued.

Kenneth Patchen's house   8.
2340 Sierra Court

This little bungalow near the end of a cul-de-sac off the Oregon Expressway was the last home of Kenneth Patchen. When Patchen died in January 1972, Lawrence Ferlinghetti wrote a moving tribute, "An Elegy on the Death of Kenneth Patchen." It begins, "A poet is born / A poet dies / And all that lies between / is us / and the world . . ."

Lew Welch's childhood home   9.
1227 Fulton Street

Although he wasn't as well known as some of the other Beats, Lew Welch was a fine poet. He was raised in the stucco house that still stands here. At Palo Alto High School, Welch became a track star and began writing poetry. When he enlisted for military service he was sent to Denver in the final days of World War II, where he became a qualified marksman. Twenty years later while visiting another dharma bum, Gary Snyder, he walked off into the forest with a gun and was never seen again. Friends searched for the body for days, but no trace of him was found. Although he wrote hundreds of excellent poems and published a dozen books, his most widely known line is "Kills Bugs Dead," the Raid insecticide slogan.

San Jose

Neal and Carolyn Cassady's house   10.
1047 East Santa Clara Street

In August 1952, Neal and Carolyn Cassady moved to San Jose and rented the eight-room house here, in what was once a nice residential neighborhood. The house is dilapidated now, but at the time it was at the edge of town and surrounded by gardens and fields. Neal was working for the Southern Pacific and this house was close enough to the railroad yards to walk to work. He grew marijuana in the backyard, but after a successful first crop, he didn't replant it, much to Carolyn's relief. Neal wrote to Ginsberg, "I got a whole closet full of weed that's grown for six months and is hanging its beautiful curly head medusa-like and downward but curled under, since its 6' and some inches length cannot come full unfurled beneath the 5 foot height of the shelf. Jack refuses to smoke (almost). Carolyn knows and satisfactorily proves to even me that it has surely made my mind fully blank, still I do get very hi, still stoned and happy, perhaps quite unhappy." In April 1953, Neal seriously injured his leg as he hopped off a freight car and he recuperated in this house. While waiting to return to the railroad, he took a job parking cars in a nearby lot. It was around this time that the Cassadys became devotees of the clairvoyant Edgar Cayce. Allen Ginsberg wrote in his diary, "Neal on the couch-divan in the living room on Sunday afternoon hand raised before his eyes in the light before the French window—holding a religious pamphlet."

Jack Kerouac visited Neal and Carolyn off and on during the three years they lived here. Jack was also working on the railroad, but the trio wasn't able to re-create the idyllic life that they had enjoyed earlier at Russell Street. In 1954 the railroad finally gave Neal $16,000 for his leg injury and with that money they bought their own house in Los Gatos.

San Jose Public Library   11.
180 W. San Carlos Street

The San Jose Public Library has moved to a new building nearby, but this old building from Cassady and Kerouac's day is still standing in the city's Civic Center and used for other purposes. In 1954 Kerouac arrived at the Cassadys' San Jose house on the all-night express freight from LA that they called *The Zipper*. He found both Neal and Carolyn obsessed with two issues: Neal's court case against the railroad and Edgar Cayce, neither of which interested him very much. He escaped to this library every day, reading Dwight Goddard's *The Buddhist Bible* and writing his own book on Buddhism, *Some of the Dharma*.

San Jose Railroad Yards   12.
White and Alameda Streets

Behind the train station in downtown San Jose are the big railroad yards where Cassady, Kerouac, and Ginsberg worked. The new arena now covers part of this area near White and Alameda. When Neal worked here, he knew the train schedules so well that he could leave home at the exact moment necessary to catch his train just as it pulled out of the yards. Ginsberg wrote a beautiful poem here: "In back of the real / railroad yard in San Jose / I wandered desolate / in front of a tank factory / and sat on a bench / near the switchman's shack. / A flower lay on the hay on / the asphalt highway / . . ." The scene is virtually the same today, although there is no longer a tank factory.

JACK KEROUAC, AL HINKLE, CAROLYN CASSADY, WITH JAMI AND CATHY CASSADY, AND MARK HINKLE. PHOTO COURTESY OF CAROLYN CASSADY

Los Gatos

The Cassady House   13.
18231 Bancroft Avenue

In 1954 Neal and Carolyn put $5,000 down on a house that stood here until recently. They should have bought the house outright because Neal lost the balance of the money they owed at the racetrack the next year. Carolyn spent the next thirty years paying off the mortgage. Here she raised their three children and wrote her autobiographical memoir, *Heart Beat*. The house and the events that took place here are further described in her delightful book *Off the Road*. In 1987 she sold the house and moved to England, and then in 1998 the house was torn down for the grander one that is now on the lot.

On one visit to Los Gatos, Kerouac went with the Cassadys to hear Bishop Romano at the liberal Catholic church. They invited the bishop over to their house to meet

Ginsberg and Orlovsky afterward. This visit from the bishop was Kerouac's inspiration for the story that became *Pull My Daisy*, Robert Frank's quintessential Beat film.

In the summer of 1956, Neal injured himself on the railroad for a second time and stayed at the house on Bancroft to recuperate even though the couple had officially separated. Then in 1957 he was arrested for possession of two joints of marijuana. When he asked Carolyn to put the house up as bail, she had to refuse, afraid he'd jump bail and the family would lose the house. Neal was sentenced to five years to life in San Quentin Prison (for two joints!). After Neal was paroled in 1960 and began seeing Anne Murphy, Carolyn filed for divorce. The railroad wouldn't take Neal back owing to his prison record and so he worked retreading tires at the Los Gatos Tire Company during his probationary period. Ferlinghetti recalls seeing him emerge bare-chested from the smoke and fumes like Vulcan at his forge.

Over the years many friends visited the house in Los Gatos. Kerouac spent a good deal of time with the family. He didn't feel comfortable sleeping inside the house, so he would unroll his sleeping bag under an oak tree in the backyard. Neal and Carolyn's son John remembers Kerouac's visits vividly—John especially liked to go out to the garden to wake Jack up early in the morning. The kids loved the neighborhood, occasionally taking Jack or Neal with them on their adventures. Once the kids "borrowed" their neighbor's go-cart while they were away. Neal jumped right on and was riding it down the street when the neighbors returned; of course they assumed Neal was the culprit, but for once he was innocent.

Los Gatos Tire Company   14.
575 University

When Neal was released from San Quentin, the terms of his parole said that he had to find a job. It was one of those catch-22 moments. The railroad wouldn't take him back and no one else would hire him because he was an ex-con. Finally he landed a menial job at the Los Gatos Tire Company, now at a different location though still in business. The workers at the place are still telling stories about Neal's escapades.

Santa Cruz

University of California at Santa Cruz Library 15.

The University of California at Santa Cruz Library has material of interest to students of the Beat Generation—large collections of poems and paintings by Kenneth Patchen and graphic works by Ferlinghetti, including drawings, lithographs, and oil paintings. William Everson, also known as Brother Antoninus, was a teacher, poet, and master printer, and his work is collected here as well.

Watsonville

Watsonville Railroad Yards 16.
South of Watsonville, just off Salinas Road

At Watsonville junction were the large railroad switching yards where Neal Cassady and Jack Kerouac caught freights and began some of their coast-to-coast trips. Sometimes Neal hung around the yards all night, usually after Carolyn had kicked him out of the house for various transgressions.

Big Sur

Edward Weston's house 17.
Wildcat Canyon, near Big Sur
(5 miles south of Carmel)

In 1956 when Allen Ginsberg and Gregory Corso were hitchhiking down the coast highway on their way to Los Angeles, they thought they'd visit Henry Miller along the way. A car left them off a few miles below Carmel and, when they couldn't get another ride, they started walking. They came to the mailbox of Edward Weston, who they knew was a photographer, and decided to visit him instead. Ginsberg records in his journal: "He was this old, old man with Parkinson's disease, in a bathrobe. . . he invited us in, we spent an hour with him, he showed us his old photos, with trembling hands took them out of drawers that were specially built to hold big enlargements." The two poets continued on their way, never meeting Henry Miller, but eventually making it to Los Angeles. Ginsberg had written in "Howl": "who digs Los Angeles IS Los Angeles."

Lawrence Ferlinghetti's cabin 18.
Bixby Canyon (12 miles south of Carmel)

The real Big Sur begins at Bixby Canyon, a half a mile inland from Bixby Bridge. Lawrence Ferlinghetti has owned a rude cabin or two in this canyon since the 1950s.

BIG SUR LITERARY OUTHOUSE.   PHOTO BY BILL MORGAN

In the sixties Jack Kerouac asked to use the cabin, hoping to kick alcohol and to get some serious writing done. Kerouac documents the failed attempt in one of his last works, *Big Sur,* in which he describes the terrible DTs he suffered. One night, alone in the cabin, he freaked out as he read Robert Louis Stevenson's *Dr. Jekyll and Mr. Hyde.* Kerouac did, at calmer moments, appreciate "the world's most beautiful outhouse."

Other visitors have included Neal Cassady, Kirby Doyle, Allen Ginsberg, Lenore Kandel, Michael McClure, Lew Welch, diverse artists, anarchists, woodsmen, and the whole City Lights workforce. Allen Ginsberg wrote his poems "Bixby Canyon" and "Bixby Canyon Ocean Path Word Breeze" on two separate visits to the cabin. Naturally, Ferlinghetti wrote many poems here. Some of them, like "Upon Reflection," vividly describe the scene. Kerouac ended his unhappy novel *Big Sur* with a fine poem that captured the murmuring sounds of the sea as it crashed onto the shore. The poem came to him when he was sitting on the beach with Ferlinghetti and asked him in his Quebecois French, "What is the sea saying?" Ferlinghetti replied in French, "There's an old Breton proverb, 'The fish of the sea speak Breton.' " Still in the tangled underbrush underneath the bridge is the old rusted car that so frightened Kerouac.

Henry Miller Memorial Library 19.
Big Sur, Highway 1
(3 miles south of Big Sur State Park)

The home of Henry Miller's friend, Emil White, on the Coast Highway has been converted into a bookstore and library named in honor of Miller. In 1944 Henry Miller settled in a little house high up on Partington Ridge, some miles south of White's place and White delivered supplies to Miller before he got his own old car. When Carolyn Cassady and columnist Al Aronowitz came to interview Miller he didn't have much time for them but he did share his insight into Kerouac's spontaneous prose theory, "That sort of thing works only in relationship to the mind behind it—if the mind is of genius, good—if not, trash." So many literary tourists came to see Miller that he posted a broadside on his gate that said he "no longer has any comfort or inspiration to offer, and that even the migratory birds avoid this spot . . . Fans and other obnoxious pests would do well to maintain silence."

Michael McClure did get past the gate, but then Miller told him, "You are an arrogant and supercilious young man, you may not stay to dinner." When a friend of Miller reminded him that he himself had once been young, arrogant, and supercilious, McClure was allowed to stay. This rejection stung McClure, as Miller was one of his early literary heroes. Allen Ginsberg wrote a postcard to Miller saying that he was coming to Big Sur and would like to drop in. Miller wrote a terse note back: "Dear Friend, please do not drop in."

Jaime de Angulo's house   20.
Partington Ridge, Highway 1 (8 miles south of Big Sur State Park)

Jaime de Angulo, the anthropologist, had a rugged stone house on Partington Ridge, a few miles south of Big Sur. Henry Miller had an Angulo-like character in "The Devil in Paradise," a story incorporated in *Big Sur and the Oranges of Hieronymous Bosch*. Miller, like many others, believed that Angulo had a streak of the devil in him.

Esalen Institute   21.
Highway 1 (15 miles south of Big Sur Lodge)

Esalen Institute was founded in 1962 by Michael Murphy, author of *The Future of the Body* and *Golf in the Kingdom,* on property that Murphy's parents had bought in 1910. It's the most magnificent setting imaginable for a center to explore human potential. A spinoff of 1960s counterculture, Esalen became known for its New Age programs combining Eastern and Western philosophies, experiential workshops, and lectures on personal libertion. Many writers held or attended seminars here, including Alan Watts and Ken Kesey. Esalen was famous even in Kerouac's day for the hot sulfur springs used by the Esselen and Salinan Indians for hundreds of years. The hot springs are open to Esalen students and faculty only, although local residents are allowed in late at night when the nude bathers are lit by candlelight.

NORTH BAY TOUR

Alan Watts's houseboat *The Vallejo* 1.
Richardson Bay, Sausalito Harbor, Gate 5

Alan Watts lived on a houseboat moored here, and commuted to San Francisco by ferry for his lectures and radio programs. Watts's *The Way of Zen, Beat Zen, Square Zen, and Zen* were on the shelves of virtually everyone in the counterculture during the 1960s and 1970s. Some critics say he oversimplified Asian religions, but his popular writings were invaluable as a bridge between East and West. In his autobiography, Watts wrote: "It had often been said, perhaps with truth, that my easy and free-floating attitude to Zen was largely responsible for the notorious 'Zen Boom' which flourished among artists and pseudo-intellectuals in the late 1950s and led on to the frivolous 'beat Zen' of Kerouac's *Dharma Bums,* of Franz Kline's black and white abstractions, and John Cage's silent concerts." Catholic Kerouac's Buddhism was certainly not frivolous, but compared to Watts's approach, Kerouac's *Book of the*

Dharma must be viewed more as "Turned-on Poetic Buddhism" than as a bridge between Western Catholicism and Far East religion.

Marin City / Mill City

Jack Kerouac and Henri Cru's shack (now demolished)   2.
Marin City exit off route 101

The large shopping center near the Marin City exit north of the city is surrounded by modern apartment buildings. These have obliterated the area where Morrisson-Knudsen built a large temporary city of barracks for employees working at the Marinship shipyards during World War II. Where the current Bay Model is located today once stood housing for 10,000 shipbuilders. When Kerouac came to San Francisco for the first time in 1947 he visited his old prep-school friend Henri Cru. Cru was working as a watchman for Morrisson-Knudsen, and he and Kerouac thought they could ship out on merchant marine ships from San Francisco. That didn't pan out, but Cru did get Kerouac a job as security guard for the barracks. Marinship had closed after the war and construction workers were living here in 1947 when Kerouac and Cru were here. Instead of guarding the property, they often ended up carousing with the construction workers and occasionally getting into trouble. In *On the Road* Kerouac wrote about his life here. In the 1960s the temporary wooden quarters were finally torn down and the ghosts of Cru and Kerouac are nowhere to be seen among the new concrete buildings.

Mill Valley

Gary Snyder's cabin and Locke McCorkle's house (now demolished)   3.
348 Montford Avenue

In 1956, before splitting for Japan, Gary Snyder stayed in a tiny unfinished cabin in the yard of Locke McCorkle. Unfortunately, the cabin at 348 Montford Avenue has since been torn down. McCorkle was a young carpenter who studied Buddhism with Alan Watts. Robert Creeley recalls that "Locke's place would have been toward the end of the road on the right, a bluff front rising up from the road quite sharply continuing on up a lot/hill to where the cabin was at the far end/top." Visitors besides Creeley included Joanne Kyger, Philip Whalen, Philip Lamantia, and Jack Kerouac. Here Snyder finished his *Myths and Texts,* and Kerouac wrote "Old Angel Midnight." On the eve of his departure, Snyder threw a giant farewell party; Kenneth Rexroth, Allen Ginsberg, Alan Watts, and others showed up to wish him bon voyage. Cal Tjader was on the hi-fi, and "in the other room wild women were dancing as Creeley of Acton Massachusetts and I of Lowell beat [drums]," wrote Kerouac. Creeley remembers "Allen and Peter charmingly dancing naked among a dense pack of clothed bodies, flowers at the prom!" The party went on for three days and nights and the nights were endless. Kerouac and Snyder took a last hike together up into these hills.

When Snyder caught a ship on May 15, 1956, Kerouac saw him off at the pier in San Francisco and gave him a little slip of paper with the line, "May you use the diamond cutter of mercy." Kerouac walked back to North Beach and spent the rest of the night at The Cellar. When the bar closed, it was too late for a bus, so Kerouac walked from North Beach across Golden Gate Bridge to the cabin in Mill Valley. He told the tale in *The Dharma Bums.*

James Broughton's houses   4
208 Corte Madera Avenue and 90 Locust

The avant-garde filmmaker, poet, and playwright James Broughton lived in Mill Valley during much of the 1960s and early 1970s. These are only two of several houses he lived in. Broughton was born in San Francisco and lived most of his life in the Bay Area, except for one long sojourn in Europe. His erotic film, *The Pleasure Garden,* made in 1953, won a special prize at Cannes the following year. Allen Ginsberg wrote that it was "on the side of the angels. It's a great testimony for love in the open." Broughton described himself as androgynous; he married twice and had two children—and also had several long-term gay relationships. His old friend, Alan Watts, described him as "the uncrowned poet laureate of San Francisco." He taught film for many years at the San Francisco Art Institute and was much loved and honored by generations of students.

Mount Tamalpais 5.
Park Headquarters off route 1

Mount Tam is the highest peak in the coast range north of San Francisco. James Broughton wrote, "We all thought of Tamalpais as a magic place. A divine place." In 1956, when Kerouac and Snyder were living in Mill Valley, they hiked the Mount Tam trails together. Kerouac describes the mountain in *Dharma Bums* as a mystic place of meditation. In the Potrero meadows, Joanne Kyger, George Stanley, Russ Fitzgerald and Jack Moore found a new way to look at the stars, by laying flat on their backs, somewhat tipsy, "with a rip in the seat of your leotards." Lew Welch wrote "The Song Mt. Tamalpais Sings," which begins, "This is the last place, there is nowhere else to go / Human movements, but for a very few, / are Westerly . . ." Even city dwellers Eileen and Bob Kaufman chose Mount Tam as the site for their remarriage ceremony on September 6, 1976.

Bolinas/ Stinson Beach

Bolinas has probably had more resident writers over the years than most large cities. At one time or another Donald Allen, Bill Berkson, Ted Berrigan, Richard Brautigan, Jim Carroll, Tom Clark, Robert Creeley, Lawrence Ferlinghetti, Bobbie Louise Hawkins, Joanne Kyger, David Meltzer, Daniel Moore, Alice Notley, Nancy Peters, Aram Saroyan, and Philip Whalen all lived in what Herbert Gold describes as the "capital of poets, artists, dropouts, sixties hippies, and feral yuppies, leavened by a few senior fifties beatniks." The Bolinas writers have mostly moved on to other parts, so perhaps the only house to mention specifically is the two-story house at number 6 Terrace Street, where Richard Brautigan committed suicide.

Richard Brautigan's house 6.
6 Terrace Street (Bolinas exit from route 1)

Richard Brautigan committed suicide in the house still standing at 6 Terrace Street. His body was discovered on October 25, 1984, but he had shot himself about a month earlier. He had alienated most of his friends and no one had noticed he was missing. David and Tina Meltzer were living here, renting the house, when Brautigan bought it. Even though he didn't intend to move in, he kicked out the Meltzer family, an act that turned even his loyal friend Michael McClure against him. He came to the empty house only rarely, and there he ended up, alone in death.

Robert Duncan and Jess Collins lived in the nearby village of Stinson Beach after Duncan quit his post as assistant director of the Poetry Center in San Francisco. William Everson also lived in Stinson Beach after he fled the Dominican order.

SAN QUENTIN PRISON. PHOTO BY STEFAN GUTERMUTH

San Quentin

San Quentin Prison 7.
I-580, San Quentin exit

In 1958, after being convicted on drug charges, Neal Cassady was sent up to San Quentin. As prisoner number A47667, his job was to sweep the floor of the textile mill. He also attended a class here in comparative religion taught by Gavin Arthur. (The two remained friends after Cassady's release, and Neal stayed often at Gavin's place in San Francisco.) Once Arthur asked Kerouac to give a talk to the prison class, but Ginsberg, eager to see Cassady, took his place. Kerouac wrote about the switch in *Big Sur.*

BIBLIOGRAPHY

Cassady, Carolyn. *Off the Road*. NY: William Morrow, 1990.

Charters, Ann (ed.). *Dictionary of Literary Biography, vol. 16: The Beats, Literary Bohemians in Postwar America*. Detroit: Gale, 1983.

Cherkovski, Neeli. *Ferlinghetti: A Biography*. Garden City, NJ: Doubleday and Company, 1979.

Cohen, Allen (ed.). *The San Francisco Oracle, Facsimile Edition*. Berkeley: Regent Press, 1991.

Davidson, Michael. *The San Francisco Renaissance: Poetics and Community at Mid-Century*. NY: Cambridge University Press, 1989.

Ellingham, Lewis and Killian, Kevin. *Poet Be Like God: Jack Spicer and the San Francisco Renaissance*. Hanover, NH: Wesleyan University Press, 1998.

Faas, Ekbert. *Young Robert Duncan: Portrait of the Poet as Homosexual in Society*. Santa Barbara, CA: Black Sparrow Press, 1983.

Ferlinghetti, Lawrence and Peters, Nancy J. *Literary San Francisco: A Pictorial History from Its Beginnings to the Present Day*. San Francisco: City Lights Books and Harper & Row, 1980.

Ferlinghetti, Lawrence. *Pictures of the Gone World*. San Francisco: City Lights Books, 1995 edition.

Fields, Rick. *How the Swans Came to the Lake*. Boulder: Shambhala, 1981.

Foley, Jack. *O Powerful Western Star*. Oakland, CA: Pantograph, 2000.

French, Warren. *The San Francisco Poetry Renaissance, 1955-1960*. Boston: Twayne, 1991.

Gebhard, David and others. *The Guide to Architecture in San Francisco and Northern California*. Santa Barbara: Peregine Smith, 1976 (2nd ed.). Salt Lake City: Gibbs-Smith, 1985 (3rd ed.).

Ginsberg, Allen and Cassady, Neal. *As Ever*. Berkeley: Creative Arts, 1977.

Ginsberg, Allen and Orlovsky, Peter. *Straight Hearts' Delight*. San Francisco: Gay Sunshine Press, 1980.

Ginsberg, Allen. *Journals Mid-Fifties*. NY: HarperCollins, 1995.

Ginsberg, Allen. *Howl: Original Draft Facsimile*. NY: Harper & Row, 1986.

Ginsberg, Allen. *Journals, Early Fifties Early Sixties*. NY: Grove, 1977.

Gold, Herbert. *Travels in San Francisco*. NY: Little, Brown, 1990.

Hamalian, Linda. *A Life of Kenneth Rexroth*. NY: W. W. Norton & Co., 1991.

Herron, Don. *The Literary World of San Francisco & Its Environs*. San Francisco: City Lights Books, 1990.

Kerouac, Jack. *Big Sur*. NY: Penguin, 1992.

Kerouac, Jack. *Book of Blues*. NY: Penguin, 1995.

Kerouac, Jack. *Desolation Angels*. NY: Riverhead Books, 1995.

Kerouac, Jack. *Dharma Bums*. NY: Viking, 1958.

Kerouac, Jack. *Lonesome Traveler*. NY: Ballantine Books, 1973.

Kerouac, Jack. *On the Road*. NY: Penguin, 1976.

Kerouac, Jack. *Selected Letters 1940-1956*. NY: Viking, 1995.

Knight, Brenda. *Women of the Beat Generation*. Berkeley, CA: Conari Press, 1996.

McClure, Michael. *Lighting the Corners: Essays and Interviews*. Albuquerque, NM: American Poetry Book, 1993.

McClure, Michael. *Huge Dreams: San Francisco and Beat Poems*. NY: Penguin, 1999.

Meltzer, David. *San Francisco Beat: Talking with the Poets* San Francisco: City Lights Books, 2001.

Natsoulas, John. *The Beat Generation Galleries and Beyond*. Davis, CA: John Natsoulas Press, 1996.

Nicosia, Gerald. *Memory Babe: A Critical Biography of Jack Kerouac*. NY: Grove Press, 1984.

Plummer, William. *The Holy Goof: A Biography of Neal Cassady*. Englewood Cliffs, NJ: Prentice-Hall, 1981.

Saroyan, Aram. *Genesis Angels*.
NY: William Morrow and Co., 1979.

Schumacher, Michael. *Dharma Lion: A Biography of Allen Ginsberg*. NY: St. Martin's, 1992.

Silesky, Barry. *Ferlinghetti: The Artist in His Time*.
NY: Warner Books, 1990.

Snyder, Gary. *Mountains and Rivers without End*.
Washington, DC: Counterpoint, 1996.

Wieners, John. *The Journal of John Wieners Is To Be Called 707 Scott Street for Billie Holiday 1959*.
Los Angeles: Sun & Moon Press, 1996.

Wolfe, Tom. *The Electric Kool-Aid Acid Test*.
NY: Farrar Straus and Giroux, 1968.

INDEX

BEAT TITLES FROM CITY LIGHTS

William Burroughs
THE BURROUGHS FILE
YAGE LETTERS REDUX

Neal Cassady
THE FIRST THIRD

Gregory Corso
GASOLINE

Diane DiPrima
PIECES OF A SONG: Selected Poems

Lawrence Ferlinghetti
PICTURES OF THE GONE WORLD: Pocket Poets #1
CITY LIGHTS POCKET POETS ANTHOLOGY
    (selections from the entire series,
    edited by Ferlinghetti)

Allen Ginsberg
THE FALL OF AMERICA: Pocket Poets #30
HOWL & OTHER POEMS: Pocket Poets #4
MIND BREATHS: Pocket Poets #35
PLANET NEWS: Pocket Poets #23
PLUTONIAN ODE: Pocket Poets #40
REALITY SANDWICHES: Pocket Poets #18
TRAVELS WITH GINSBERG: A Postcard Book

Jack Kerouac
BOOK OF DREAMS
POEMS ALL SIZES: Pocket Poets #48
SCATTERED POEMS: Pocket Poets #28
SCRIPTURE OF THE GOLDEN ETERNITY:
    Pocket Poets #51

Philip Lamantia
BED OF SPHINXES: Selected Poems

David Meltzer
SAN FRANCISCO BEAT: Talking with the Poets
    (interviews with 13 Bay Area poets)

Also Available

THE BEAT GENERATION IN NEW YORK
A Walking Tour of Jack Kerouac's City

Edited by Bill Morgan

Set off on the errant trail of the Beat experience in the city
that inspired many of Jack Kerouac's best-loved novels
including *On the Road*, *Vanity of Duluoz*, *The Town and the
City*, and *Desolation Angels*. This is the ultimate guide to
Kerouac's New York, packed with photos of the Beat
Generation, and filled with undercover information and
little-known anecdotes.

978-0-87276-325-5
$12.95